Gagan Syal

AF239006

CAE - PROCESS AND NETWORK

A methodology for continuous product
validation process based on network of
various digital simulation methods

Reihe Informationsmanagement im Engineering Karlsruhe
Band 2 – 2013

Herausgeber
Karlsruher Institut für Technologie
Institut für Informationsmanagement im Ingenieurwesen (IMI)
o. Prof. Dr. Dr.-Ing. Dr. h.c. Jivka Ovtcharova

Eine Übersicht über alle bisher in dieser Schriftenreihe
erschienenen Bände finden Sie am Ende des Buchs.

CAE - PROCESS AND NETWORK

A methodology for continuous product validation process based on network of various digital simulation methods

by
Gagan Syal

Dissertation, Karlsruher Institut für Technologie (KIT)
Fakultät für Maschinenbau
Tag der mündlichen Prüfung: 3. Mai 2013
Referenten: Prof. Dr. Dr.-Ing. Dr. h. c. Jivka Ovtcharova
Prof. Dr.-Ing. Kristin Paetzold

Impressum

 Scientific
Publishing

Karlsruher Institut für Technologie (KIT)
KIT Scientific Publishing
Straße am Forum 2
D-76131 Karlsruhe

KIT Scientific Publishing is a registered trademark of Karlsruhe
Institute of Technology. Reprint using the book cover is not allowed.

www.ksp.kit.edu

Print on Demand 2013

ISSN 1860-5990
ISBN 978-3-7315-0090-2

CAE - PROCESS AND NETWORK:

A methodology for continuous product validation process based on network of various digital simulation methods

A Doctoral thesis to obtain the Degree of
Doktor der Ingenieurwissenschaften (Dr.-Ing.)

for submission to the Faculty of
Mechanical Engineering
of Karlsruhe Institute of Technology

DISSERTATION
By
M.Sc. Gagan Syal

First Doctoral Advisor: Prof. Dr. Dr.-Ing. Dr. h. c. Jivka Ovtcharova
Second Doctoral Advisor: Prof. Dr.-Ing. Kristin Paetzold
Day of vocal examination: 03 05 2013

Preface of the Publisher

Computer aided engineering (CAE) describes behavior of products and simultaneous validate a product design. From scientific and practical viewpoints, these simulation methods have to be executed and synchronized in a process considering their interdependencies. For instance while performing car's door digital validation, various simulations have to be performed e.g. fatigue, crash, forming. According to interdependencies, crash simulation needs output of forming simulation as an input which authenticates a need of CAE process. So far, most of the simulations are performed in an isolated way using pre-results or hardware test results as input. Besides using such inputs digital simulation and current results are mostly available. Due to unavailability of CAE Network and methods to import inputs from various dependent sources, it reduces quality of simulation results. As a consequence, CAE process has been accomplished partially and in a manual way, which make engineers unable to validate a system in faster and efficient way.

Thus, a new methodology to develop CAE network considering interdependencies among digital validations is developed in this work. Utilizing the CAE network and considering industrial requirements, an algorithm is applied to enable a product, vehicle development phase, and load case priority oriented CAE process. The methodology is validated using an application CAE-ProNet which is developed. Motive of this application is to provide practical guidance of the methodology for simulation engineer, method engineer, process engineer and manager. The CAE network by means of generic relation matrices helps to reduce complexity of managing simulation data. The CAE process helps to improve quality of digital validation and simultaneously reduces time-to-market by decreasing dependencies on hardware prototype. Motorhood is used as a first business use case to validate the methodology and the methodology is implementation in civil structures to validate wider usability. Major advantage of this research work is to improve quality of simulation by developing computer aided network of CAE methods.

Prof. Dr. Dr.-Ing. Dr. h. c. Jivka Ovtcharova

Karlsruhe Institute of Technology

Acknowledgement

This dissertation is the results of my research work carried out at Daimler AG, Ulm from Oct 2008 to Sept 2011 as doctoral candidate. The work was incorporate with Institute for Information Management in Engineering (IMI) at Karlsruhe Institute of Technology (KIT).

First and foremost, I would like to express my gratefulness to my doctoral thesis supervisor, Prof. Dr. Dr.-Ing. Dr. h. c. Jivka Ovtcharova (Head of Institute for Information Management in Engineering) for her academic support, encouragement and having interest in the work. From the very first day her guidance and support was with a clear direction. This perfectly helped me to be on right track of the thesis. Simultaneously, she was very open to new ideas that were sometime out-of-the-box. Her guidance to contact other researcher in her institute accelerated and broadens the research work. I am grateful to Prof. Dr.-Ing. Kristin Paetzold for her academic support and being a member of the evaluation committee.

Many thanks to my managers Mr. Robert Winterstein, Mr. Bernd Ehrenberg, Thomas Krumenkar and Prof. Dr. Christian Glöggler those continued to assist and evaluate my work. I sincerely thank my colleagues and friends Dr. Rainer Ostermayer, Dr. Alexa Nawottki, Mr. Martin Gottwald, Mr. Simon Königs, Mr. Vincent Tixier, Mr. Dharmeshkumar Sheta, Mr. Vipin Garg, Mr. Varun Sharma, Mr. Khandwekar, Mr. Sen, Mr. Son Vo and Mr. Walla, Dr. Michael Prieur who supported and encouraged me on every step.

For the practical approach, I was in continuous touch with various CAE teams. Without the inputs and feedbacks of CAE engineers, results wouldn't be to optimal. I hearty thanks all CAE engineers who were involved the work. Special thanks to Dr. Andreas Ruf, Dr. Christian Glandier and Dr. Mark Eiselt for their precious time they spend on my projects and thesis work.

Finally I am grateful to Mr. Nick Suyam for the endless time and marvelous effort he spends with me from structuring to finalizing the work, and Karuna (my wife) for her remarkable support.

Gagan Syal

Table of Contents

List of Abbreviations

CAE - Computer Aided Engineering

FEA - Finite Element Analysis

CFD - Computational Fluid Dynamics

VVRL - Validation to Validation Relation Library

NVH - Noise, Vibrations and Harshness

MBS - Multi-Body Simulation

FSI - Fluid-Structure Interaction

SDM - Simulation Data Management

PDM - Product Data Management

GUI - Graphical User Interface

VDP - Vehicle Development Process

OEM - Original Equipment Manufacturers

DSM - Design Structure Matrix

CAE-ProNet - Computer Added Engineering – Process and Network

FVM - Finite Volume Method

FEM - Finite Analysis Method

List of Figures

List of Tables

1 INTRODUCTION

1.1 Motivation and Challenges

More than 125 years of automobile history, automotive industry passed through various peaks and valleys. Innovation has always been the key to success for any car manufacturer and it set to become even more important at present and in future. Race to be first in innovation and developing high tech products is one of the major challenges of companies. To develop such products which are characterized by the integration and interplay of complex mechanics, electronic, and

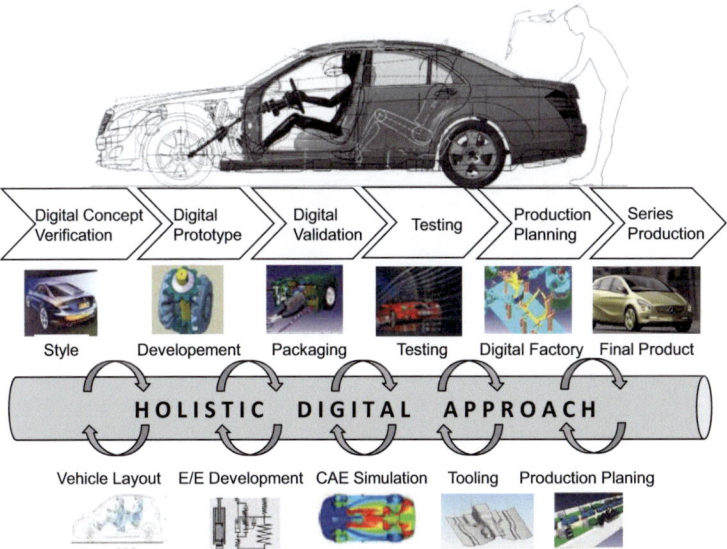

Figure 1. 1 Holistic Digital Approach for Product development

software components a holistic approach of vehicle development and production is vital.

The motivation to develop high technical products that satisfy increasing customer requirements on style, quality, comfort, safety, cost and environment protection, is pushing all OEMs (Original Equipment Manufacturers) to work on holistic digital approach from the concept phase to the final phase (as shown in figure 1.1). [Söre-06] [SySu-11] [Thom-98]

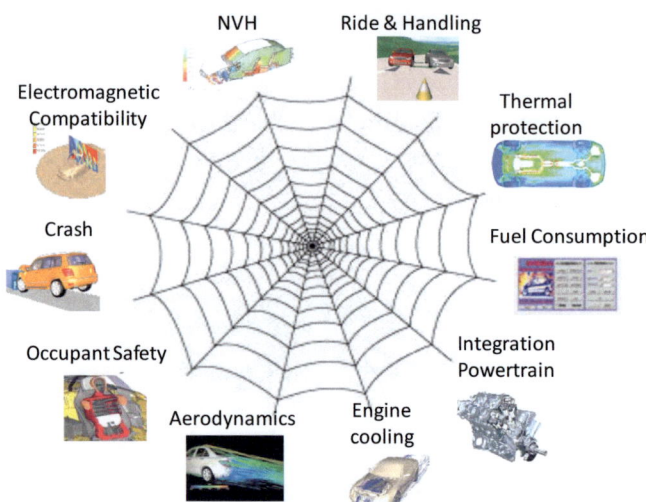

Figure 1. 2 Network of Computer Aided Engineering

In VDP (Vehicle Development Process), digital validation approach is CAE (Computer Aided Engineering) that makes it possible to simulate almost all aspects of the product's behaviors in a virtual environment. To validate a product numerous validation methods like stiffness analysis, fatigue analysis and fluid analysis are used. Moreover, within a same domain, different simulation tools are used. Currently in automotive industry, there is an inefficient interaction among validation methods. The motive to build CAE network is one of the objectives of this research work (Figure 1.2).

Inputs required to validate a product for CAE are to some extend dependent on hardware prototypes. E.g. to calculate noise level on the occupants of the vehicle, one has to perform NVH simulation. Indeed, NVH (Noise, Vibrations and Harshness) can be caused by several sources, from vehicle itself as well as from external environment.

One of these sources is wind which acts as distributed forces. Currently pressure loads due to wind are calculated and imported from wind tunnel. The pressure loads can also be provided from aerodynamics simulation but these testing results are used due to unavailability of CAE Network. This leads CAE system to be dependent on hardware prototypes in automobile industry (as shown in Figure 1.3). Moreover, hardware results are available at later stages of vehicle developments process.

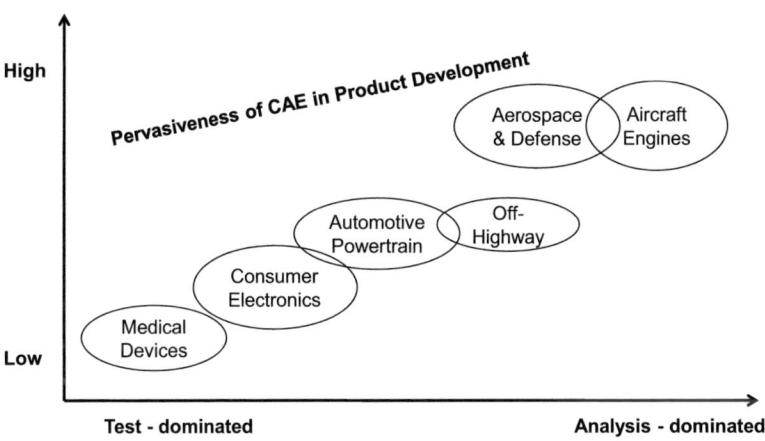

Figure 1. 3 CAE Pervasiveness in Industries Studied [JeBr-06]

At early stage of development process, simulation engineers have to use testing results of previous car. There are solutions in the area of multidisciplinary and co-simulation but factors that define relation between simulations and factors of relation are not well distinct in digital world. There is a demand of single platform where each validation can distinguish factors which affect their validation methods to validate a particular product on a specific VDP phase. [Ausi-08a] [Hann-11] [SpBe-11] [ScRa-11]

Figure 1.3 illustrates pervasiveness or occurrence of CAE in product development in various industries. CAE systems are majorly in aerospace and defense. Due to high expenses and time consuming testing in aerospace, aerospace industry is more dominated to CAE than testing. Small products and medical industry is still dominated to testing. Automotive is pushing itself to be more in CAE and applying more and more digital methods. [JeBr-06]

1.2 Objectives

This dissertation is designated to perform a research approach to optimize CAE system. The objects of investigation are automotive body in white, exterior parts, vehicle development phases and interfaces. Indeed, relation between CAD, CAE and CAM in VDS is necessary but this research is concentrated only to CAE-CAE relation. The major objectives of this research work are described as follows:

Objective 1: The first major objective of this thesis is to collect factors defining a relation among CAE simulations and developing a method to build CAE Network.

This thesis aims to analyze all relevant theoretical factors or data sources along vehicle development process in order to identify relation among CAE. Due to increasing number of components, variants and front loading targets the number of simulation and load cases increases exponentially. Thus, to reduce complexity of holistic system and validating that system requires a systematic approach that achieves a collaboration of CAE methods throughout the life cycle of system. Therefore, it can be ascertained that new methods are necessary in order to support various CAE domain in a vehicle development process.

The factors to network CAE methods have to be defined with higher level of granularity and data collected is a library of relations among CAE simulations. The CAE network can be independent of product. Thus, the CAE Network could be applicable in various workgroups and organizations.

Objective 2: The second major objective is to devise an algorithm to describe a product, phase and priority (or combination of all) oriented CAE Process derived from CAE Network.

Further objective is systematization of CAE process according to their downstream process requirement like product, development phase and load case priority oriented simulations. The challenge to describe a dynamic process which could be effortlessly altered according to dynamics requirements during development phases. To integrate the CAE Process in existing VDP (Vehicle Development Process) is one of the objectives and complexity depends on number of simulation and load cases in an organization. In this context it is aimed to provide solution with minor modification in existing structure. The final process helps to improve the understanding of product and system validation from concept to final validation phases.

The purpose of optimization of CAE process chain is to develop the structure of digital backbone for the connection of various simulations. Key emphasis is a holistic and integrated data model which is used to describe individual processes and facilitate the communication among them. In order to achieve these objective, requirements to share the information and knowledge of all simulations is vital along PLM (Product Lifecycle Management). Therefore, solutions are integrated to Simulation Data Management.

Objective 3: Finally, feasibility of theoretical principles and system concepts is to be piloted in such a way to provide practical guidance for simulation engineer, method engineer, process engineer and manager by means of a digital solution i.e. CAE-ProNet application.

Further challenge is to implement a new paradigm in existing business process, taking into account an organization structure and philosophy as well as knowledge and work diversity of users. "CAE-ProNet" application presents know-how of the methods implemented and structured in this thesis work. Furthermore, the application is aimed to provide a digital backbone for the end users who are simulation-, method-, process engineers and as well as managers.

1.3 Expected Advantages

The expected benefits of the research carried out for this thesis are as follows:

1.3.1 Enhancement in CAE result quality

Computation results are always estimated and by continuous development in CAE methods it increases results quality. By means of CAE Networking, inputs received to dependent simulation are in detailed form as compared to simplified or assumption based simulation. Thus results carried out by using thesis methods are expected to be of better approximation and closer to real results.

1.3.2 Team collaboration

CAE teams often work in isolation. Indeed, they received parts from CAD teams for validation and design improvement but very seldom they linked to other simulations. Data exchange among CAE teams positively builds team collaboration. This results in fewer simulation errors, increased repeatability of CAE with traceability.

1.3.3 Flexible and Transparent

The product and system responsible get a complete look on dependencies. Such processes offer opportunities to speed development progress by streamlining the inter-task coordination.

1.3.4 Improved CAE System

Managing complexity of CAE and its processes is always a major challenge. Aftermath of thesis work includes that the system responsible get an overview about all relevant simulations, dependencies, mapping and processes of his responsible system. Dynamics CAE process provides up-to date progress of CAE process and quality of simulation results. Thus, it will be easier to control and track CAE System which helps managers to take decision within development process.

1.3.5 Reducing dependencies on Hardware Prototypes

The methodology results in constructing CAE network which assists dependent simulation to use the digital results of its dependent simulation. Thereby, it reduced the dependency on Hardware prototypes.

1.3.6 Cost

The aim of this thesis is to provide methods and processes to support the product development process. The results improve the quality of simulation and reduce the dependency on hardware which affects in reducing cost of development.

1.3.7 Reducing redundant CAE and mapping tool

One of the aftermaths of CAE network is reduction of redundant mapping tools. Due to lack of single platform, each department uses their own experience and standards for CAE. This results in using various CAE tools for same discipline. Moreover, for mapping process departments build their own mapping application or buy commercial tools. This research will help organizations to identify and reduce redundant CAE and mapping tools.

1.4 Focus of Investigation

This thesis work is focused to CAE systems, vehicle development process and simulation data management in the field of automotive exterior and interior parts.

1.4.1 CAE System

There are various perception of Computer-aided engineering (CAE) by different researchers. For example Ernst G Schlechtendahl from Kernforschungszentrum Karlsruhe says *"CAE comprises several disciplines of computer application to engineering problems. From a systems analysis point of view, the different stages of the development of a new product may be mapped on to disciplines such as computer-aided design, computer-aided manufacturing, and others"*. S.A Meguid says – *"CAE is a term embracing the related areas of Computer aided design (CAD), computer aided analysis (CAA), and computer integrated manufacturing (CIM)."* In Industrial world CAE means digital validation or analysis which is also known as simulation. [Schl-85][Megu-87]

In this research work CAE means *"a method to determine digitally the behavior of product"*. CAE system includes digital validation system, CAE process and simulation data management".

1.4.2 Vehicle Development Process

Importance: High (1) Medium (2) Low (3)	Medical Device	Consumer Electronic	Auto Power train	Off-High way	Aero / Defence	Aircraft Engine
Support for analyst/engineer needs for right data fast	1	1	1	1	1	1
Corporate knowledge capture, retention	1	1	1	2	1	1
Global CAE data sharing, reuse	1	1	1	2	1	1

Managing intra-CAE data flows	3	2	1	1	1	1
Managing CAE/CAD data flows	3	2	1	1	1	1
Managing CAE/test data correlation	2	2	1	2	2	2
Support for systems-level/whole-product simulation	3	2	1	1	1	1
Collaborating with partners, subcontractors, suppliers	3	3	2	3	1	2
Protecting IP in CAE outsourcing	3	3	2	2	2	2
Building, managing materials data libraries	2	1	2	3	3	3
Managing manufacturing data needed for simulation	2	1	2	3	3	3

Table 1. 1 The value of applying CAE in early design process

Vehicle development Process (VDP) is a series of action taken to bring a vehicle to market. The initial phases are focused on identifying customer requirements and converting them to specifications and functions of each vehicle system. CAE System and simulation Data management is an integrated part of VDP

Spar Point Research [Table 1.1] survey highlight that the importance of getting right data fast is high in automotive sector. For simulation engineers, data can be CAD model, material properties, inputs from dependent simulations and many more. Getting the right data and analyzing the right data is indeed an additional challenge. Collecting and maintaining CAE know-how is on high demand so that it can be used globally. Data sharing and reusing helps to work efficiently and reduce repetitive efforts. [JeBr-06] [JeBr-07]

A wide range of technologies are used during different design phases in simulation driven product development, including structural finite element analysis, acoustics, crash applications, fatigue and failure analysis, and computational fluid dynamics. When CAD geometry is available during design refinement and function evaluation (Table 1.1), it is used to validate simulation results against tested physical prototypes. The report is based on Spar Point's research in digital validation at aerospace/defense, aircraft engine, automotive Powertrain, consumer electronics, medical device and off-highway equipment manufacturer. [Nits-05][Raca-09]

1.4.3 Simulation Data Management:

As simulation data volume is growing and time taken to extract right information for an engineer increases exponentially. Without simulation process and data management simulation engineers spend 30% of their time in searching for data (figure 1.4) [ScSt-10].

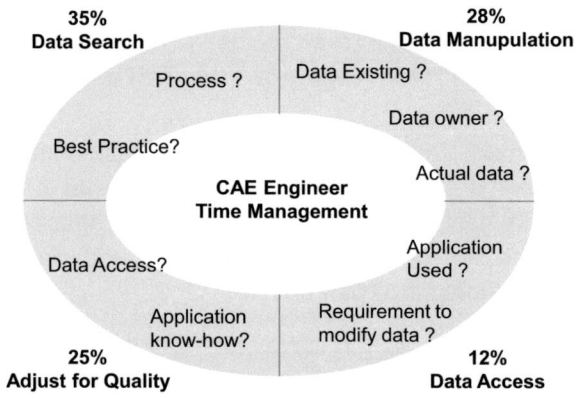

Figure 1. 4 Time management of Simulation Engineers [ScSt-10]

Simulation engineers use individual team data management for their data. It has many limitations as data is not sharable. Moreover, data flow is unidirectional from organization data backbone to teams as shown in figure 1.5. To solve such challenges, CAE Team management or called Simulation Data Management is introduced.

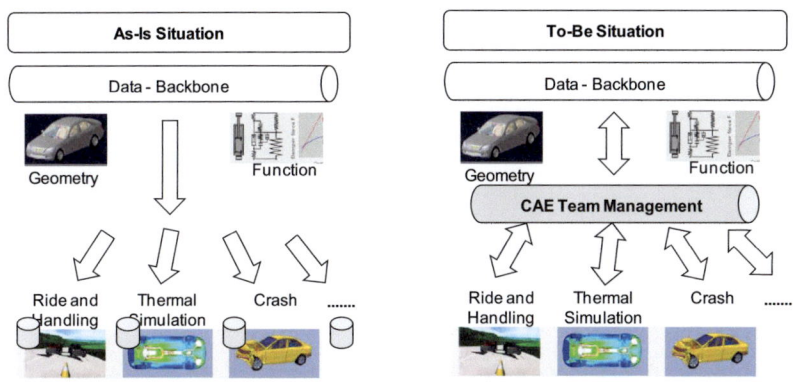

Figure 1. 5 As-Is and To-Be Situation of Simulation Data Management

One of the requirements of simulation data management is to manage inter-CAE data flows, corporate knowledge capture and retention, and receiving simulation engineer input data faster. All these requirements are focuses of this research work. [YaJi-04][Kutz-02]

1.4.4 Automotive interiors and exterior parts:

Another focus of investigation in this thesis is automotive body and exterior parts e.g. motorhood, doors, roof. The attractiveness of a car body increases importance of exteriors body parts validations. Thereby the number of load cases to sustain the internal and external requirement increases significantly which helps to investigate and validate the thesis results in this areas. The scientific goals are divided as follows:

Methodology: Capturing, structuring and processing of digital validation phase.

Systematization: Structuring validation methods in the form of an intelligent semantic, ontology bases framework that integrates various digital validations.

Implementation: Digital solution that integrates in existing processes.

1.5 Definitions

Product: A "product" is to mean a tangible output that is engineered as result of a process and that is intended for delivery to a customer or end user. Product Design in general is defined as the idea generation, concepts development, testing and manufacturing of a physical object. Thus, product Designers conceptualize and evaluate ideas, making them tangible through products. The idea of a product arises from a need and has a use (for example function or behavior). [Sama-08a] For Example: Motorhood; Doors; Seats; Brake etc.

Component: Assembly of small components lead to a product. For Example: Motorhood is a product and its components are outer structure, internal part (Body-in-white), reinforcements, Front Hinges, Damper; etc.

System: Assembly of products lead to a system. For Example: Fuel System, Drive train etc.

Simulation: In simulation, causes are applied to particular structures in order to observe effects (or more precisely, behaviors). For example, a factory process is simulated to observe output and other aspects, such as sensitivity to breakdown of a machine. [Raph-03]

Analysis or Load case: It a special case of simulation also known as load cases. Analysis is performed when behavioral parameters are required for a given physical configuration in a particular environment. For example bridges are analyzed for various loading (such as wind, truck and earthquake) in order to determine behavior that is expressed in terms of stresses and deflections. [Raph-03]

Verification: It is the process of determining that the fundamental behaviour of a simulation is consistent with the fundamental laws of motion, energy conservation and momentum. Verification of a model establishes that the physics of the simulation are correct. [Ausi 08b]

CAE Network: A group or system of interconnected and non-interconnected Simulation.

CAE Process: A "process" consists of CAE activities, a sequence of CAE operations that are planned and executed in accordance with policies. A CAE process involves relevant stakeholders who monitor, control, review and evaluate described process. A series of interdependent simulations carried out with respect to time. [Sama-08a]

Workflow: the sequence of industrial, administrative, or other processes through which a dependent simulation passes. It is of two types: sequential and parallel.

Vehicle Development Phase: distinct period or stage in a process of change or forming part of car development.

Interpolation: Interpolation is the procedure of estimating the value of properties at unsampled sites within the area covered by existing observations and in almost all cases the property must be interval or ratio scaled. [MaBu-04]

Mapping: A mapping is a model that relates the objects (attributes) of two other models; each object in a mapping in a mapping is called "mapping object" and has three properties: domain and range, which point to objects in the source and target respectively, and an expression that defines the semantics of that mapping object.[SeLu-05]

Motorhood or Bonnet: The hood or bonnet is the hinged cover over the engine of motor vehicles that allows access to the engine compartment for maintenance and repair. On passenger cars, a hood may be held down by a concealed latch.

1.6 Outline of the Thesis

This thesis is structured in six parts as shown in figure 1.6. After this initial chapter, state of art is described. The approach of this research work is to fulfill the current industrial requirements using scientific methods and procedures. Chapter 2 is divided into two parts: first parts "State of Art – Industrial" is to understand existing industrial systems. This chapter is devoted to figure out the challenges in system that can be solved. Another part is "State of Art – Scientific" in which the existing solution or approach are elaborated.

After getting familiar with challenges and existing system know-how, a new methodology is described to solve highlighted challenges. Chapter 3 begins with discussing detailed objectives for the new methodology CAE-ProNet. This closed loop methodology starts with problem identification approach. The approach helps management in decision making for the execution of CAE-ProNet methodology. A theoretical approach to specify dependencies among simulation is explained in this

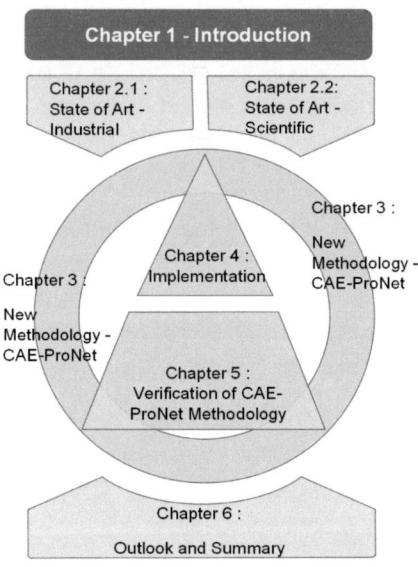

Figure 1. 6 Thesis Structure

chapter. On the bases of this theoretical approach, an industrial solution to build Network of simulation and its process is provided. Major functionalities to build a digital solution of CAE-ProNet are elaborated. Finally, the chapter contains added- values follows by chapter summary.

Representation of each block in below given figure 1.6 has significance to its content like chapter 2.1, chapter 2.2 and chapter 6 support chapter 3, 4 and 5. Chapter 3, 4 and 5 are closely integrated as CAE-ProNet methodology is described and elaborated using examples in chapter 3. The methodology is continuous and closed loop that why it is represented by circle.

Implementation of complete methodology to build a digital solution (CAE-ProNet Application) that can be integrated in existing systems within organization is performed. User Interfaces for each user groups are explained. The chapter continues with further requirements to build new and improved version CAE-ProNet application and finally ends with chapter summary.

Chapter 5 is planned to verify the methodology in practical. This chapter follows the steps of CAE-ProNet described in chapter 3 using CAE-ProNet application illustrated in chapter 4. An Automotive business case is use to validate the CAE-ProNet methodology.

Final chapter 6 "Outlook and Summary" contains further areas of investigation. It includes how other industries like Bio-medical, aerospace can use the CAE-ProNet to improve current system. Finally, the summary contains essential results obtained in this thesis and thesis is enclosed with a conclusion.

2 STATE OF ART

2.1 Introduction

Networking and sharing information through software have become common practices in all OEMs. To compete in a global economy, companies are using various methodologies to concurrently collaborate on design and simulation challenges. Stricter environmental regulations impacting profit of automotive industry. On the other side, automotive market growth is increasing worldwide especially in BRIC countries

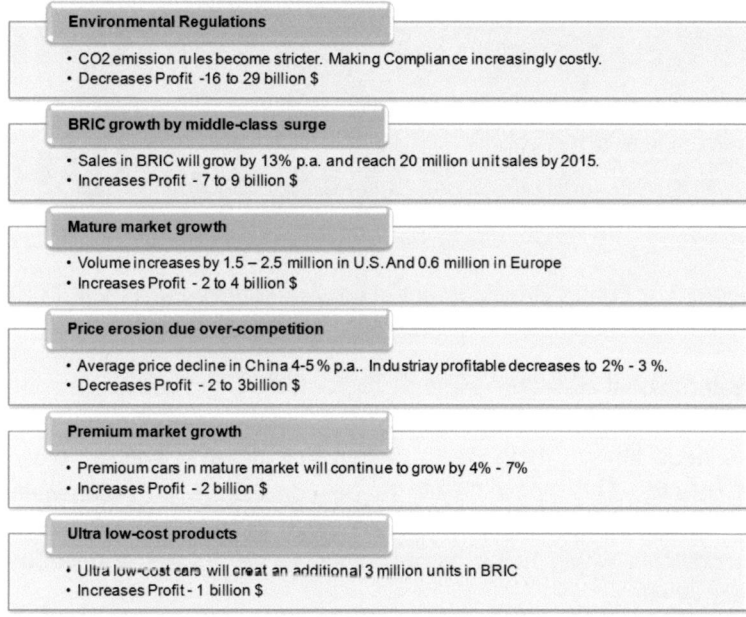

Environmental Regulations
- CO2 emission rules become stricter. Making Compliance increasingly costly.
- Decreases Profit -16 to 29 billion $

BRIC growth by middle-class surge
- Sales in BRIC will grow by 13% p.a. and reach 20 million unit sales by 2015.
- Increases Profit - 7 to 9 billion $

Mature market growth
- Volume increases by 1.5 – 2.5 million in U.S. And 0.6 million in Europe
- Increases Profit - 2 to 4 billion $

Price erosion due over-competition
- Average price decline in China 4-5 % p.a.. Industriay profitable decreases to 2% - 3 %.
- Decreases Profit - 2 to 3billion $

Premium market growth
- Premioum cars in mature market will continue to grow by 4% - 7%
- Increases Profit - 2 billion $

Ultra low-cost products
- Ultra low-cost cars will creat an additional 3 million units in BRIC
- Increases Profit - 1 billion $

Figure 2. 1 Automotive Megatrend [HeMa-11]

(Brazil Russia India China) as shown in figure 2.1. [HeMa-11] [IFF-10] [Delo-11]

This results in tremendous global automotive component growth. During recession in 2009, automotive components market was 417 billion Euros, in 2012 it's 527 billion Euros and expected to be approx 663 billion Euros in 2020. For Example, Indian (one of BRIC countries) passenger car market has almost 4 times within a decade. The growth rate of care sale and production were 15.8% and 17.6 respectively for the period between 2001 and 2010. [HeMa-11] [MAI-10] [StBr-12]

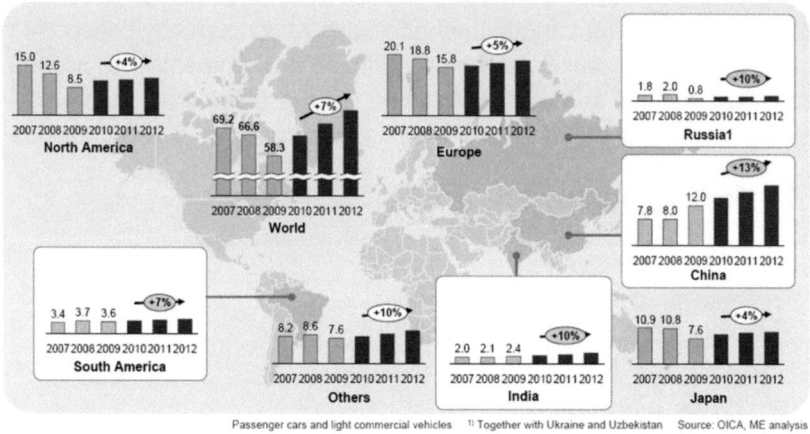

Figure 2. 2 Future Development in the Automotive Industry [IFF-10]

Illustrated global statistics evidently highlights the growth of automotive industry in BRIC Countries. To fulfill the requirement of new markets OEMs need holistic methods to design and develop specific parts in each country. This helps OEMs to be competitive for local market. Thus, this growth directly impacts the need of new technologies and methodologies which helps organizations to be quicker and better in global market.

2.1.1 Objective

The objective of this chapter is to illustrate existing requirements and challenges in scientific and industrial CAE world. To understand and elaborate the challenges, three major areas a) CAE Network, b) CAE Process and c) CAE Data management are selected. Even though these areas are interlinked but to figure out challenges at each level of system these areas are separated.

For the evaluation of existing methods and tools, following features are taken into consideration:

- Identifying CAE interdependencies

- Handling comprehensive CAE complexity

- Adapting and customizing dependencies

- Improving traceability and transparency of CAE System

- Improving accuracy of CAE results

- Supporting in reduction of hardware prototype

The Chapter - State of Art has been divided into two parts. First part is "State of Art – Industrial" which is focused to methods and processes currently used by automotive companies. Second part is "State of Art – Scientific" which explains the scientific existing and ongoing research projects in the same area. Both parts include CAE Network, CAE Process and CAE Data Management. The final evaluation define the requirement of a new methodology and it's described in session "Chapter Summary".

2.2 State of Art – Industrial

In automotive industry, there are many facets of challenges to execute simulation process and simulation data management. Isolated, less time for simulation in development process, various simulation types, lack of inter disciplinary knowledge are major challenges in CAE

System. Due to tremendous numbers of simulations involved in automotive sector, number of dependency among simulations increases exponentially. The dependencies among simulations are often overlooked which ends up in decreasing simulation accuracy.

Importance of system understanding and validation can be recognized by following examples "Consider Toyota's sudden acceleration problem. Before that, the Ford-Firestone tire blowout problem. And in an entirely different industry, the BP-Deepwater Horizon oil spill in the Gulf of Mexico. Each of these cases involved physical phenomena in complex systems. Each involved multiple physical properties and mutiphysics domains. Each could have undoubtedly been better understood with more computer-aided engineering (CAE) and simulation. But there's a catch. More simulation increases the complexity of simulation management, organizing and making sense of the simulation results, and making simulation data available to people (corporate and regulatory) and to other information systems (applications and data repositories, on-site and remote, within a company and with partners and vendors)." [LaGo-10]

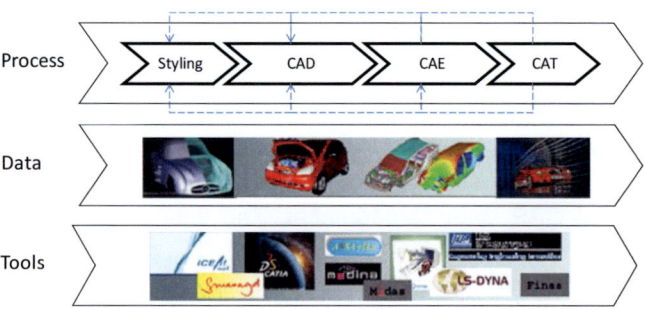

Figure 2. 3 Integration in Vehicle Development Process [NaAl-09]

To understand any system process, data and tools have same importance in vehicle development process of any organization. Information exchange among CAD CAE etc plays inquisitive role in holistic system development approach. High demand to manage CAE

Intra data work flow is specified in research surveys as in Table 1.1. Simultaneously, there is requirement of managing CAD-CAE data flow. Continuous editing process in CAD models due to CAE and other way around CAE models have to be changes as per CAD. Therefore, to manage the data work flow between them is of high importance. Moreover on the whole data flow among styling, CAD, CAE and CAT is a major challenge in today's car development process as in figure 2.3. The solution of these challenges is to make more efficient use of existing resources like software tools, engineers, etc. [NaAl-09] [SIMD-06] [SCAI-06]

This research work is concentrated to the relation among CAE disciplines. Thereby, state of art industrial and scientific portray CAE networking techniques, CAE processes and CAE data management.

2.2.1 CAE Network

Daimler AG

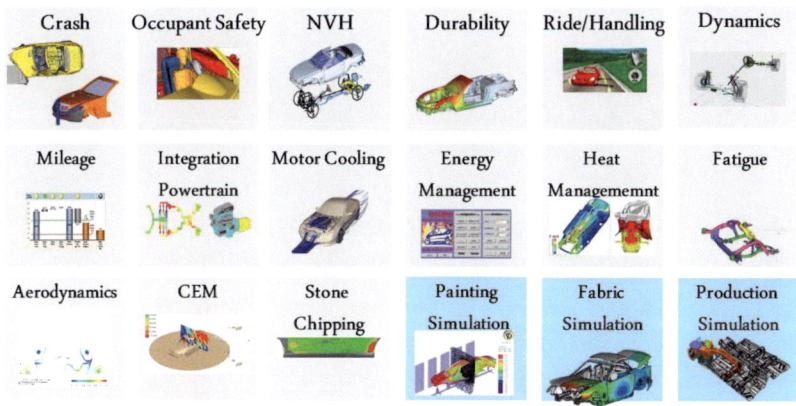

Figure 2. 4 Major Simulations in Automotive Industry [KaAl-07]

Daimler AG (www.daimler.com) is having a vast field of simulation methods. As shown in figure 2.4, Daimler does occupant safety, durability, crash, aerodynamic simulation etc. Some simulations are related to production like painting process simulation.

A final product comprises of various processes and manufacturing steps. Such products pass through various physical changes. On the contrary, in digital world, simulation methods are often used to optimize each single process step. Hence, if a result of a simulation has an influence on another simulation it requires a dependent data transfer. For example in figure 2.5 a process chain is described with an influence of cold rolling on forming and forming on crashing. At Daimler AG, Mr. Sebastian Lossau in corporate with Prof. Bob Svendsen (TU Dortmund) work on digitalizing this process. [LoSv-09]

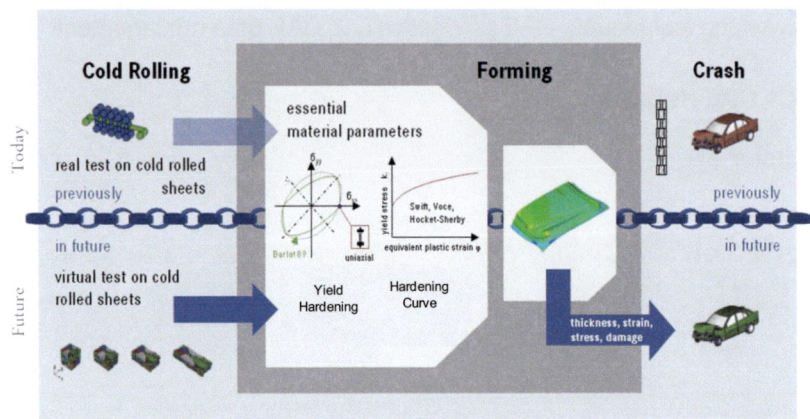

Figure 2. 5 Simulation Process Chain [LoSv-09]

As shown in figure 2.5, now a day's outcome of forming simulation i.e. thickness, strain distribution, stress and damage are not used in crash simulation. Due to this the simulation accuracy is reduced. To overcome these digital results of forming can be directly exported to crash simulation. Similar way, for forming simulation material properties are inputs and these inputs are received from real testing results not from digital or virtual test. Thus forming simulations are dependent on hardware testing. To eliminate hardware dependencies such dependencies are identifying and companies require CAE Network.

Indeed, Daimler's CAE department runs efficiently but there are vast heterogenic challenges. Some of them are described as follows:

- Different modeling methods for FEM, MBS, CFD and FVM are used which leads to non standardization. In development process dependent simulations are not able to get know-how of data they received as input.

- Different model requirement (mesh size, element size etc): Drastically changing requirements increases the complexity of uniformity and standardization.

- Different tools for pre-post and solving: Each simulation requires a specific tool and even of similar FEM simulation different tools are used.

- Deficiency of CAE Network leads to non transparency of simulation system.

- Lack of methods to identify interdependencies among CAE.

- Lack of methods to identify similar FE-model that can be common or re-use.

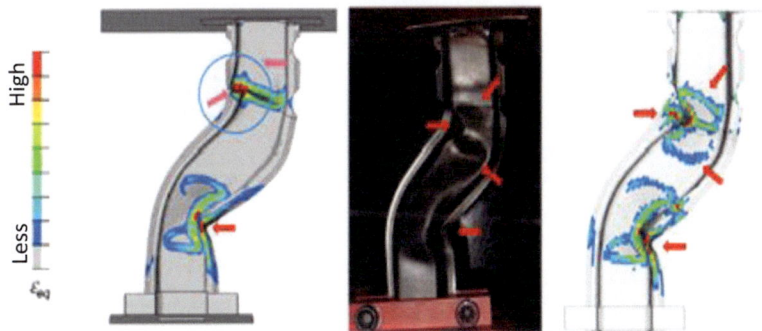

Figure 2. 6 Comparison of crash simulation results of non-mapped (left), mapped (right) with experimental crash test (middle)

Advantage of CAE Network to improve simulation accuracy is demonstrated in figure 2.6. A crash simulation is done including forming results and without including forming results. Outcome of using forming results is compared to experimental hardware test and found more realistic than non mapped results. This simple example demonstrates the enhancement of simulation quality results by CAE Network.

Conclusion of CAE Network at Daimler is that various methods, requirements, tools, sequences and simulation steps are used in Daimler. Deficiency of CAE Network leads in inaccessible of simulations to each other. Simultaneously, it results in reducing simulation quality or to some extend results in product design failures. [KaAl-07] [NeBi-09] [NeFe-08]

Evaluation results of each OEM for CAE Network are summarized in Table 2.1. There was no feature which could identify inter-dependencies. CAE Network examples were individual cases and were identified by simulation engineers as per their requirement. Existing CAE Network were feasible to handle comprehensive CAE complexity. Existing methods can partly applied through the organization. Indeed existing CAE Network helps to improve quality of result but it's difficult to adapt and customize dependencies with existing methods. Dependencies among simulations are apparent which open-up necessarily of CAE Network for the organization.

Audi

Some examples of CAE- Network at Audi are given in this session. To simulate CAE complex structure (at AUDI AG) like of airbags, engineers need fast computer to simulate FSI (fluid-structure interaction). Algorithms in PAM-CRASH 2G software require supercomputer for high resolution model and are used in AUDI. [RoAm-08]

Audi strategy for virtual handling and ride dynamics is integrated with VI-Grade. To build the mechanical vehicle modeling ADAMS car handling model ADAMS Car ride model, VI-CRT (Car Real Time) and

Matlab models are used. It is used to collect inputs for VI-Suspension and VI-Driver and Model are exchanged using sockets or files. The challenge is to simulate the model in real time. The basic workflow of the model is shown in figure 2.7. [WiMi-09] This model is a comprehensible example of MBS CAE-Network.

Moreover, Audi uses Dymola for multi-domain vehicle dynamics simulation .Mechatronic system (mechanical, electrical and software) simulation is done in one tool i.e. Dymola which opens ways for simulation of hybrids and electric drive trains. By means of mutiphysics simulation, cosimulation and workflow among simulation, Audi and BMW are step ahead to other mentioned OEMs. [DeGe-10]

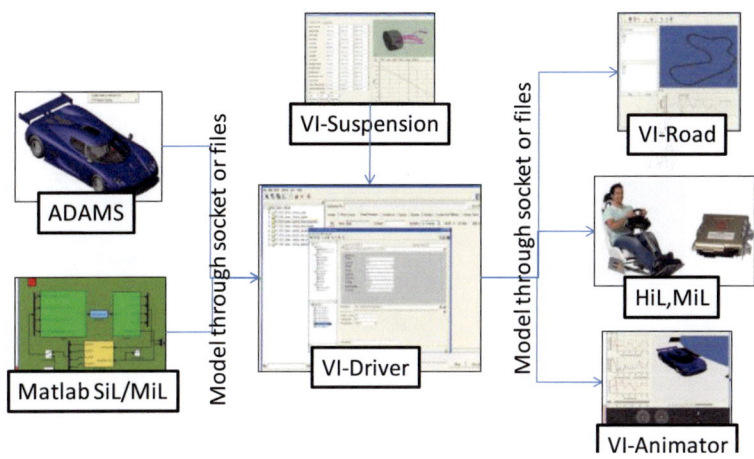

Figure 2. 7 Work Flow of VI - Car Real Time [WiMi-09]

BMW

BMW engineers use Simpack for Multi Body Simulation. SIMPACK is a 3D Multi-Body simulation software which is used to aid engineers in analysis and design of mechanical and mechatronic systems. Multi-Body Simulation of Powertrain Acoustics in the Full Vehicle Development to calculate interior noise level for occupants, simulation engineers need various excitation forces. In concept phase it's difficult to get details excitations. Using SIMPACK, BMW does the concept design of Powertrain acoustics in the full vehicle development. [ScAl-11]

In given figure 2.8, Simpack model is having an approximate 150 DOF (degrees of freedom). It contains Subsystems (Powertrain Model +Rear Axle Model +Engine/Roller Excitation), Rigid Body (Base Version), Tire Model, Friction in Powertrain and Rear Axle, Nonlinear Characteristic and Amplitude-Frequency Rubber Characteristic.

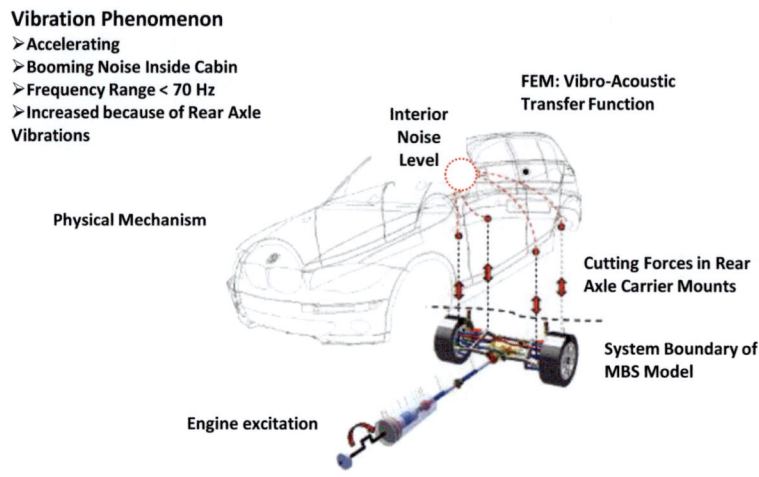

Figure 2. 8 Multi-Body Simulation of Powertrain Acoustics using SIMPACK [ScRa-11]

The advantage elaborated by BMW on Multibody simulation is that it shortens development time. SIMPACK, and the modular approach used at BMW, have made it possible to implement this complex multi body simulation. For realistic driving experience of new vehicle concepts on the ride simulator, a validated MBS-method is essential. The validation with measurements shows a precise correlation to the MBS-simulation. This gives a very high quality of forecasts in reviews. [ScRa-11]

GM - Opel

Opel started using a combination of ANSA (used for Surface Grid/mesh) and Fluent (Computation fluid dynamic) tools to simulate fluid flow or flow field around a vehicle.

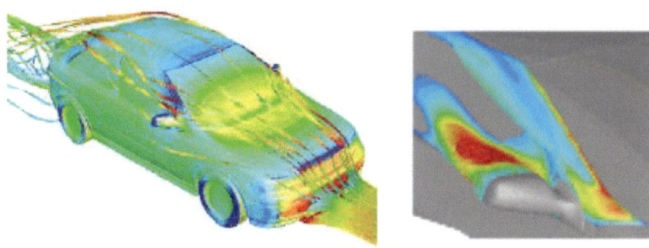

Figure 2. 9 Flow Visualization: Pressure distribution on vehicle exterior (left) and near A-Pillar (right) [KlAn-01]

Wind Tunnel test for flow visualization is time consuming, outputs are limiting and expensive. On other side, CFD simulation generates detailed information for entire flow field. Flow field visualization (E.g. surface pressure) supported by path lines can provide lots of information regarding behavior of product and optimization areas. In addition, aero-acoustics information is extracted which is used to analyze turbulence energy distribution or the progression of wall surface streamlines in the A-Pillar region and at the side glass. Figure 2.9 (right) shows the flow field visualization and Figure 2.9 (left) explain pressure distribution at A-Pillar region.

The pressure distribution is used as an input for durability simulation engineers. This CAE Network at GM - Opel elaborates dependency between Aerodynamics and Stiffness analysis. [KlAn-01] [Ansa-98] [Flue-97] [SpGS-94] [PiCh-95][ArKr]

Toyota

Toyota Research Institute of North America reviewed mutiphysics optimization of thermal-fluid structures using COMSOL and MATLAB. Heat transfer and fluid flow effects logically produce different 'optimal' results. The optimization method can be applied to a broad variety of vehicle applications. Other physical systems are also currently being explored using COMSOL Mutiphysics simulation e.g. electromagnetic applications. [DaGa-2012]

The evaluation results are collect in table 2.1. Evaluation is done as per feature feasibility. Rating is divided into 5 parts. -1- When the feature is accomplished completely and in use. -2- When the feature is accomplished partially and some of the part is in use. -3- When only basic of that feature is accomplished and in use.-4- When feature does not exist and finally -0- for not-relevant feature for that particular files.

1 - Feature accomplished 2 - Feature partly accomplished 3 - Feature basically accomplished 4 - Feature not accomplished 0 - Not relevant		Feasibility to identify CAE interdepend-encies	Feasibility to handle comprehens-ive CAE complexity	Feasibility to adapt and customize dependencies	Feasibility to improve traceability and transparency of CAE system	Feasibility to improve accuracy of CAE results	Feasibility to support reduction of hardware prototype
State of Art - Industrial							
CAE Network	Daimler	4	2	4	3	2	2
	Audi	4	2	3	2	2	3
	BMW	4	2	4	2	2	3
	GM-Opel	4	3	3	4	3	3
	Toyota	4	3	4	3	2	3

Table 2. 1 Evaluation of Industrial CAE-Network

2.2.2 CAE Process

VDP (Vehicle Development Process) made great stride towards the description of workflow and timeline. Interdisciplinary domain's workflow is comprehensibly depicted in VDP. The CAD department has to finish responsibilities and handover CAD models to CAE department on freezing dates. The workflow between these domains and data transferring is a standardized process.

Phases and functions are clearly defined. Activities of each discipline are specified with time line. As in figure 2.10, the development system contains Product Development, Marketing System, Administration, Sales, Production system, After Sales, and Quality Control.

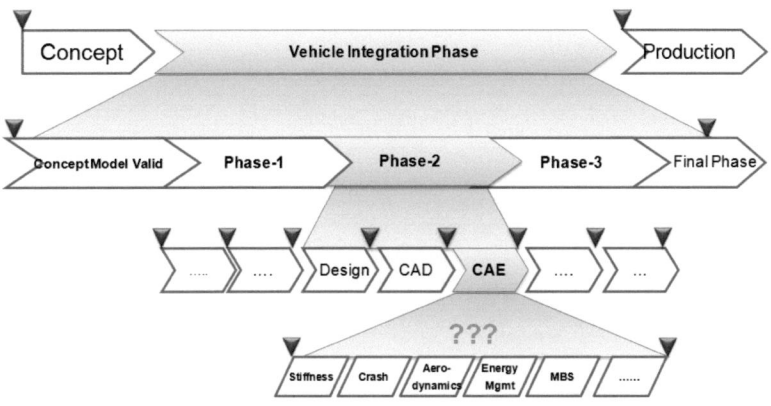

Figure 2. 10 Vehicle Development System

Narrowing to CAE domain in development system, it includes various kind of digital validation methods like stiffness analysis, Crash Analysis, Aero-dynamics etc., there is a requisite of standardized data flow between each other. Currently the data flow is executed manually and partially which results to an error prone and time-consuming process. Indeed, there is a vital requirement of a CAE process which must be integrated in VDP. Presently in most of the industries, a CAE process is a parallel process as shown in Figure 2.11. Each digital validation execute independently to the other even though they are working on same product. Some processes and solution help to network validation methods but not enough for the complete CAE domain. In exception of parallel process, crash and durability simulation of Body-in-white is done in early steps.

After getting CAD model CAE departments start working parallel in spite of having dependencies towards each other. E.g. while validating the stiffness of a car's front glass stiffness analysis engineers need the results (pressure distribution) from Aerodynamics. This states that the Stiffness analysis engineers have to start after the Aerodynamics engineers completed their tasks. Existing methods are manually or partially manually operated and are not efficient for the complete CAE process.

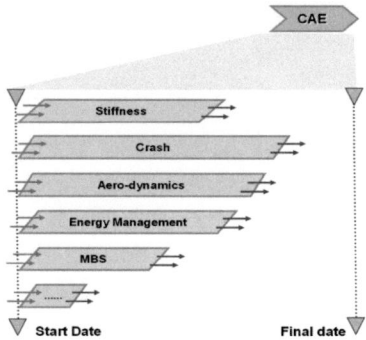

Figure 2. 11 CAE Process

The consequences due to the deficiency of CAE process are as follows:

- Difficult to co-ordinate the large and versatile CAE structure.

- No controlling on deadlines.

- No standardized simulation data workflow.

- Manual process results to an error prone and time-Consuming process.

- Unable to validate complete system.

- Dependent on Hardware testing (a time consuming and expensive process)

On the contrary, if the workflow among simulations are in sequential form than it results in extension of vehicle development time which is inadequate according to the development process. Time Factor plays a major role in describing and optimizing a CAE process. The solutions of these challenges are well described later on.

Daimler

Daimler AG product concretization allows to appropriate phase of project to secure Mercedes Benz quality. Each phase of vehicle development includes designing and validation of that design by simulation and physical testing. In earlier phases (or concept phase) existing of design and validation is more. As the development proceed activities of design and validation decreases as shown in figure 2.12.

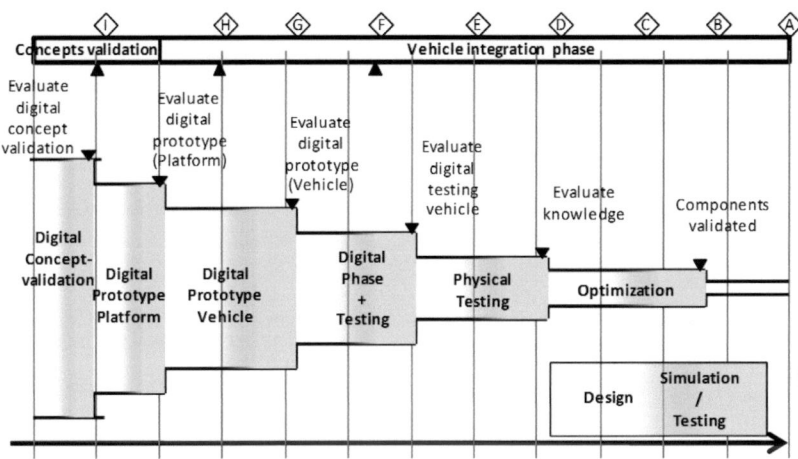

Figure 2. 12 : Efficient Creativity: Process and Methods in Automobile Industry [LaRa-11a]

Commercial simulation process tool like SimManager offer solutions to structure the process but does not identify or highlight interdependencies. All dependencies have to be defined manually by simulation engineers. Moreover, traceability and customizing features of interdependencies are still at same place. CAE Process requires dynamic behavior that can be edited within development process and shows process for granularity level.

To structure a system, process engineers have to define Input data, process execution data, output data and finally linking them manually. Therefore, there is a necessary requirement of a CAE process that describes workflow among various CAE departments as per theoretic or/and practical dependencies. [LaRa-11b]

Audi

Audi AG, occupant safety system for frontal impact is developed using finite element simulations. The number of load cases in this discipline increases to 26 over last years. To make it as automatic the occupant safety simulation must meet the following requirements. a) Transparency and traceability must exist to review the status of selected or all load cases and b) Customization, optimization and editing of system can be easily done.

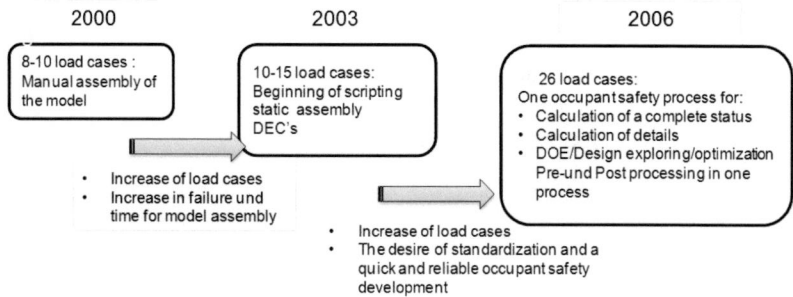

Figure 2. 13 Timeline of automated process for occupant safety simulation development [HoMl-06]

A tool named "Variator" form Audi AG is programmed which includes the above listed requirement [HoMl-06]. The evolution of this process at

Audi is displayed in Figure 2.13. Audi CAE-Bench is used at AUDI as simulation management which is a cutting edge simulation system. The system helps AUDI to increase 6 times as throughput, expended from 9 to 35 model lines and expanded simulation into multi-discipline. More information is in section 2.1.3 [Norr-10]

BMW

Similar to Audi, BMW AG is using CAE-Bench System for CAE Process and data management. In Figure 2.14, process automation is described where the CAD data for Digital Mockup is imported in CAE Process. This CAE process can be automated in CAE-Bench where modeling assembly, solving, key results and reports are generated using standard templates. The BMW system increases CAE system transparency. Automated CAE process aids in reducing hardware prototyping. [ScTh-10]

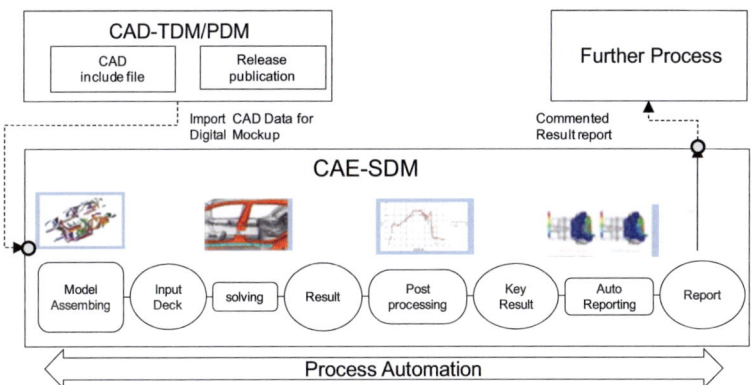

Figure 2. 14 CAE Simulation based on Simulation Data Management [ScTh-10]

GM - Opel

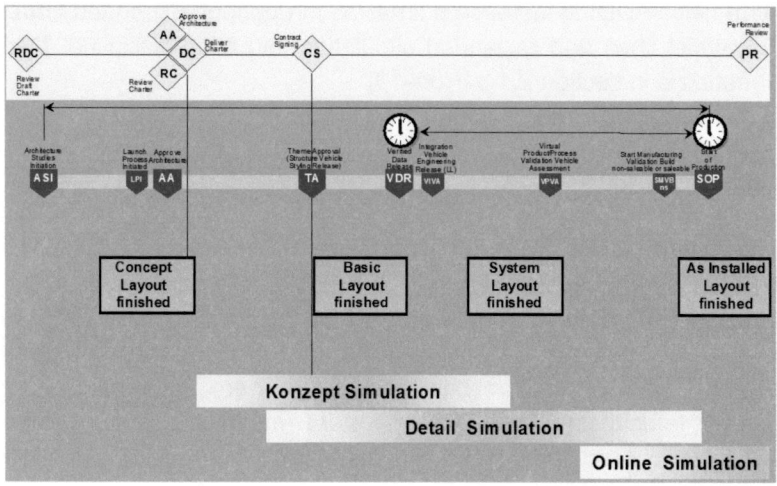

Figure 2. 15 General Motors Leadtime model and
Simulation process

The process in GM/Opel is given in Figure 2.15 and figure 2.16. It is
divided into three various categories – concept, details and online
simulations. Online simulations are executed via batch mode and ideal
for repetitive load cases for optimization. The goal is to have process for
individual simulation. After overall assessment, simulation models and
reports are integrated into full vehicle. In this type of CAE process the
inputs for supplier are given by OEMs. The inputs are major tasks,
guideline (method of simulation), software and milestones. Suppliers
takes these as inputs and delivers Simulation models, model validation
and reports which helps OEMs for product / part assessment as per
requirements.

These CAE process highlight process with supplier and helps to
simulate individual products. Indeed the process is fast but not ideal to
integrate full vehicle especially while networking it with other
simulations.

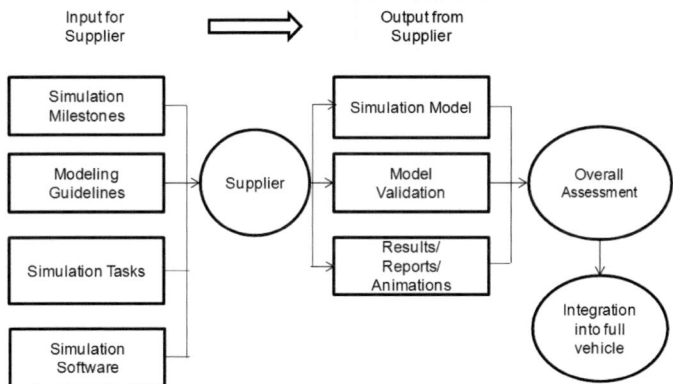

Figure 2. 16 CAE Process at GM [TeLo-07]

Toyota

Toyota Motor engineering and manufacturing North America aimed to establish a seamless process to evaluate Powertrain design for mount vibration and radiated noise. The major advantage is reduce calculation time and improve simulation accuracy.

Scopes for Powertrain dynamic analysis are

- Applying multiple software (MSC Nastera → AVL-EXCILE → MSC NAstran → LMS Virtual Lab (Sysnoise))

- Time consuming simulation which evaluates single design

- Requires evaluation of various engine operating conditions

- Requires parameter sensitivity controlling for simulation accuracy.

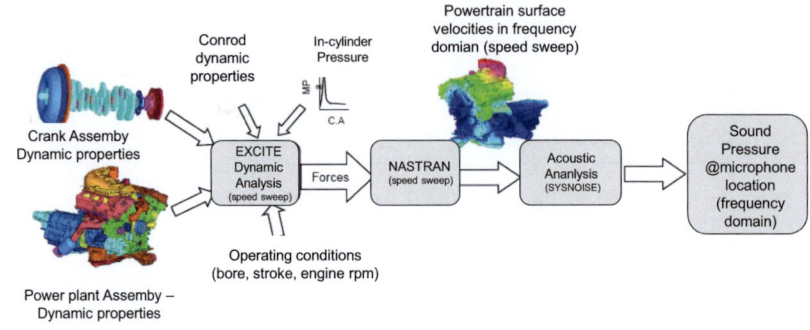

Figure 2. 17 Toyota Dynamic Analysis Process [DeLi-09]

To calculate dynamics analysis for speed sweep, inputs from various resources like Crank Assembly, Conrod properties etc are collected. After dynamics analysis using inputs and operational conditions, output forces aids in calculating surface velocities in frequency domain. This leads to measure sound pressure at defined locations with higher accuracy and in lesser time.

1 - Feature accomplished 2 - Feature partly accomplished 3 - Feature basically accomplished 4 - Feature not accomplished 0 -Not relevant	Feasibility to identify CAE interdepende-ncies	Feasibility to handle comprehens ive CAE complexity	Feasibility to adapt and customize dependencies	Feasibility to improve traceability and transparency of CAE system	Feasibility to improve accuracy of CAE results	Feasibility to support reduction of hardware prototype
State of Art - Industrial						
	Daimler	0	3	3	3	0	0
	Audi	0	1	2	2	0	0
CAE Process	BMW	0	1	2	2	0	0
	GM-Opel	0	2	3	2	0	0
	Toyota	0	3	3	2	0	0

Table 2. 2 Evaluation of Industrial CAE Process

The outcome of CAE process reduces calculation time from 20-25 days to 2-3 days. Improved sound pressure level results accuracy. The dynamics analysis improves simulation accuracy and opens further improvement scope of engines design optimization using similar process. [DeLi-09]

The CAE Process state of art is evaluated and summarized in table 2.1.

2.2.3 CAE Data Management

CAE Data Management challenges are not same as of CAD or Electric Data Management. The primary reason is because CAE and simulation databases are huge compared to others. Figure 2.18 demonstrated an increase of CAE data in Mercedes Benz. In 2002, the number of crash simulation per vehicle increases to 500 and volume of C-Class simulation data was 2139 GB. There's data about pressures, temperatures, material properties, boundary conditions, solver algorithms used, and many more.

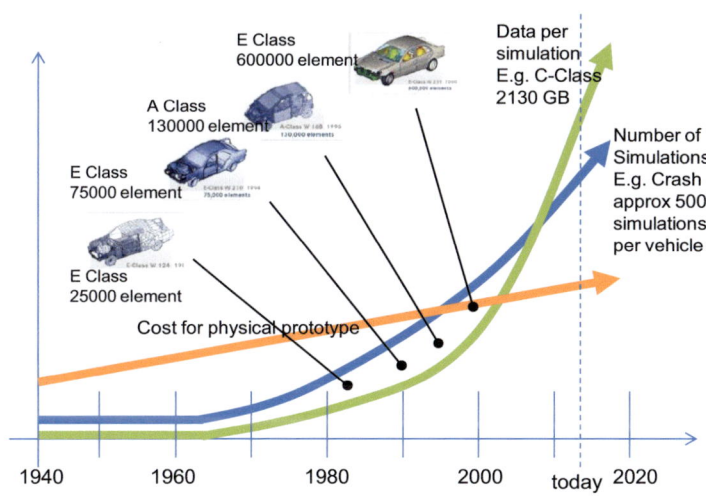

Figure 2. 18 CAE Data Growths

On everyday bases, the basic problem is in storing simulation data and making those data accessible. Scott Del Porte, lead product manager for Ansys EKM at Ansys, Inc. (ansys.com), ticks off some other effective

CAE data management benefits: *"Accessing and reusing historical design information and expertise to aid in the progress of new designs. Capturing and leveraging existing engineering knowledge. Addressing the loss of engineering expertise, while protecting intellectual property. Reducing future development costs and risks by simulating a wider range of operating conditions."* [GoLa-10] [More-11] [Muel-12] [Mill-09]

Daimler

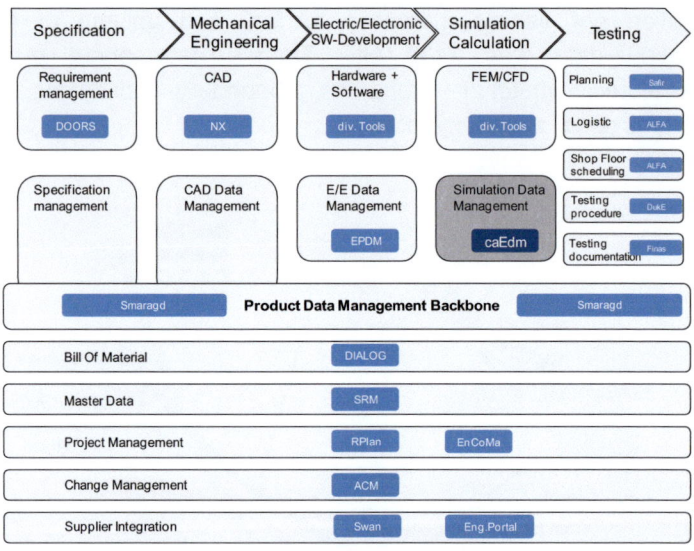

Figure 2. 19 Daimler existing and upcoming IT-Processes and System [KaAl-11]

Daimler continuous development plan of major IT Processes and System are given below in figure 2.19. Daimler plans to shift its CAD system from CATIA to NX and it is in pipe line. New development projects are applied using Siemens – NX CAD system. Similarly for simulation data management, customized Siemens Teamcenter tool is used and known as "caEdm".

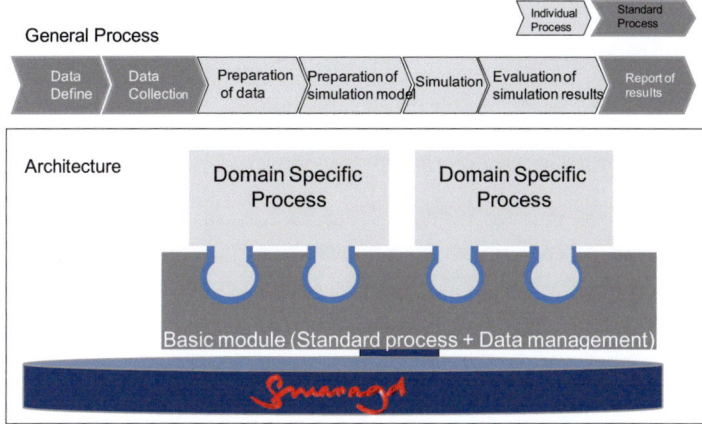

Figure 2. 20 Daimler caEdm - Process and Architecture

The goal of caEdm is an implementation of an efficient and standardized CAE-Data management for all Daimler process. There is a string increase in complexity and number of projects at Daimler. Thus, it increases the requirement of simulation data management. "caEdm" has been planned in January 2008 and first release of Basic Module of caEdm was planned in 07/2011 [KaAl-08] [KaAl-11]

Currently, team data management is used which is applicable for individual teams. T-Systems' customized data management tools - MIDAS Pre and MIDAS Post are used in Daimler. In fact these tools are efficient for distinct teams but do not work at comprehensive level of large scale OEMs.

The concept of caEdm is to support all CAE domains and is structured as a) A base module in which common function used by all CAE domains are implemented and b) A set of Domain Modules in which domain specific functions are implemented.

The key results and benefits of caEdm are:

- Support Daimler's "Digital Prototype (DPT)"

- Allow multiple use of CAE data

- Transparent documentation of CAE Results

- Support workflow for more automation

- Integrate individual results for system evaluation

After evaluating various software architecture for caEdm, Daimler goal for caEdm is to have single data management for all teams. The caEdm is integrated to Daimler PDM System. Other architectures are illustrated in below pictures. [Keln-10] [Daim-12]

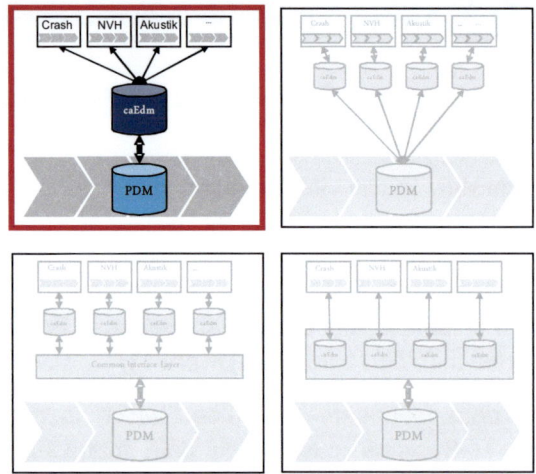

Figure 2. 21 Daimler Architecture for caEdm

Audi and BMW

Audi and BMW are using CAE-Bench based on SimManager as a Simulation data and process management. Such systems reduce regular tasks from analysts by restructuring the data and process. Currently, most of the data is still managed by moving flat files and organizing them in directory structures. In addition, most of the processes in pre- and post-processing are not standardized and the obtained simulation results are not very consistent between individual studies. The results can thus not always be compared directly; since it has to be examined manually to which extend the data was generated consistently. Due to this current situation the simulation experts spend a considerable amount of time with administrative tasks of documenting simulations, preparing standard reports and communicating key results to process partners.

With the CAE-Bench project the focused on addressing these aspects and designed a web based system for managing the simulation data, generating a standard reporting process and providing a consistent information system for the process partners. In addition to the pure data management of simulation results, there is an additional long-term focus, the Knowledge Management. Each individual simulation performed in a car project represents a large number of information, however in the context of the individual study only specific functional characteristics are important and analyzed.

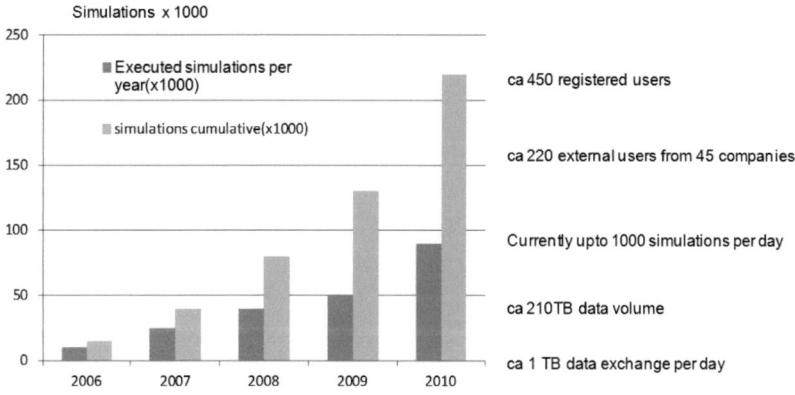

Figure 2. 22 Audi CAE-Bench Tool Statistics

Many additional insights are neglected. With CAE-Bench data ware house was built, which holds the simulation data from pre- and post-processing for all simulations performed in an organization. These dataware households in some encoded form a huge amount of knowledge obtained through simulations. With data mining approaches it will be possible to extract this knowledge, which should then lead to new insights and hereby, even further improves the car design process. [Schl-10] [Norr-10] [MSC-12]

BMW Group and MSC.Software have agreed to jointly develop a CAE Automotive Portal to replace the BMW "CAE-Bench" simulation data management solution. SimManager Automotive Portal will be included as an additional solution in MSC.Software's product portfolio during 2011. [John-10] [BMW-12] [MSC-12]

GM-Opel

In less than 10 years of implementing Teamcenter as Global Data Management and Access, General Motors multiple its users to 40 times and access from 29 sites in 15 countries. This global data management is not included simulation data. GM pilot project to built simulation data management was started in late 2007.

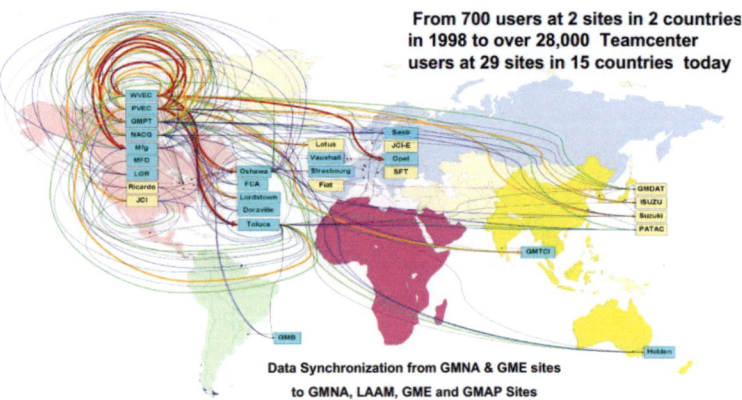

Figure 2. 23 General Motors - Global Data Management and Access

The goal is to support non-geometric data, re-use, process automation, remote job submission, robust design and integration with other (PLM) system. Besides that CAE dependencies are one of the major requirements in SDM. GM strategy is based on Math Based synthesis Driven. In Past, hardware-based vehicle development and Hardware-driven analysis support was in practice. However now and even more in future, virtual product development and synthesis-driven simulation are performed.

General Motors, Daimler, VW and other OEMs use Teamcenter as Data management. Extending its usability for simulation plays a key role. As operating IT tools from a unified database have numerous benefits. The single data model also makes data mining and integration with ERP easier. It links seemingly various system parts. Ideally developing a holistic system using unified data base is principal requirement at General Motors.

From various sources, it gives the impression that General Motors has no Global Simulation Data Management till now.[Mein-07] [Cafe-09] [Goud-08]

Toyota

Information Technology has not been a first priority for the people and process at Toyota. From 2001, however, it became a high priority to the company. Afterwards within 4 years company spent 200 billion Yen on Total Information System for Vehicle Development (TIS). Toyota has strategically decided to develop its own PDM system in-house. Such efforts have proven to be a major challenge for other OEMs including Toyota.

At present, digital development system expended and integrated across CAD CAM CAE and CAT and CAPP (Computer Aided Process Planning). Subsequently, Toyota Motors deployed Windchill from PTC (www.ptc.com) as the platform for CAD data management and product lifecycle management (PLM) at its Powertrain division. The target is to establish a multi-CAD environment with a single bill of materials (BOM). Astonishingly, CAE and simulation represent a second priority at Toyota with heavy funding in hardware side alone. [PTC-12] [Brow-07][Burk-04]

1 - Feature accomplished 2 - Feature partly accomplished 3 - Feature basically accomplished 4 - Feature not accomplished		Feasibility to identify CAE interdependencies	Feasibility to handle comprehensive CAE complexity	Feasibility to adapt and customize dependencies	Feasibility to improve traceability and transparency of CAE system	Feasibility to improve accuracy of CAE results	Feasibility to support reduction of hardware prototype
State of Art - Industrial							
CAE Data Management	Daimler	3	4	4	2	0	0
	Audi	3	2	3	1	0	0
	BMW	3	2	3	1	0	0
	GM-Opel	4	4	4	4	0	0
	Toyota	4	4	4	4	0	0

Table 2. 3 Evaluation of Industrial CAE Data Management

2.3 State of Art – Scientific

Over last decades many domain-specific simulation tools have been accepted and widely used (such as MATLAB/Simulink or Dymola for multi-physics modeling, SystemC for Electronics, ASCET for automatic control engineering or Flowmaster for thermal simulations). However, in most cases these tools are often tailored for individual physical areas. Thus, they tend to be focused to limited heterogeneous simulations, which are described in previous section "State of Art – Industrial". This section "State of Art – Scientific" is dedicated to the research projects that are ongoing or completed.

2.3.1 CAE Network

AUTOSIM

AUTOSIM (Sept 2005– Aug 2008) is a project funded by the European Commission within the 6th Framework Program. The project was a successor to the FENet project (www.fe-net.org), focusing on the automotive sector. Automotive companies (Renault, PSA Peugeot Citroen, Volvo etc), Software companies (Abaqus, Enginesoft, CAEvolution etc) and research institutes (Arsenal Research, Uni Manchester etc) were involved in this project.

Major Key technical areas were a) Integration of CAE into vehicle development process and b) improving use of simulations. Multi-physics simulation and Multi-disciplinary optimization (MDO) technology were also covered in integration into development process.

The summarization of AUTOSIM research work is as follows:

- Current coupling tools are concentrated to major two disciplines – structural analysis and computational fluid dynamics. But a vehicle should have been tested by simulation for a combination of concurrent factors, such as occupant safety, multi-body simulation and fatigue. The outcome results suggested proceeding in the areas of Multi-Physics and Multi-Disciplinary Optimization.

- In future, CAE and CAE data management have to be taken into consideration for distributed development environments in PLM. Tools and Processes must be integrated (including Suppliers) as per knowledge and resources.

- Simulation data management will be used to store and retrieve data. Tools should be set in place to take advantage of knowledge gained from analysis runs from designs of car predecessors, or from previous analysis runs of crash, NVH, durability, etc.

The outcomes of the project emphasize the requirement of integration of simulation and need of simulation data management in PLM. [AUTO-08] [EUCAR] [Kues-07]

Modelisar

Modelisar research project was funded by ITEA 2 (Information Technology for European Advancement) from July 2008 to December

2011. Automotive companies like Daimler, VW, Volvo were partners in this project. DLR, Fraunhofer, Uni Halle were research partners and software associates were Dassault System, Simpack, LMS etc.

The purpose of Modelisar is to develop functional mock-up (FMU) with new methods, standards and tools to support holistic design: Holistic design for simulation and test of systems including embedded software.

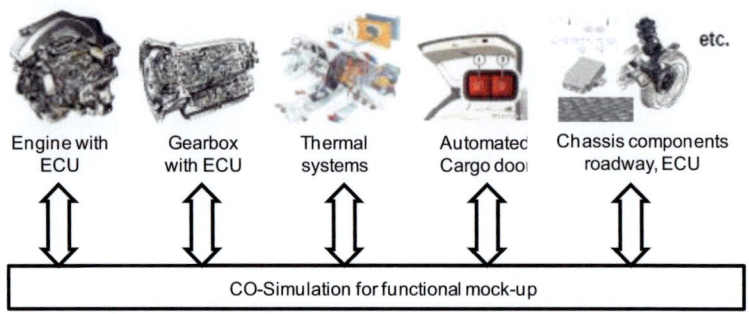

Figure 2. 24 Modelisar – Functional Mockup-Up

Traditional co-simulation platforms are usually limited to few domains, e.g. calculation of thermal management system or communication architecture with a heterogeneous set of tools. With that it is possible to simulate sub-systems, but difficult to get simulate whole system.

The major objectives of MODELISAR are 1) to enable concurrent design of embedded systems and software. The research is to use existing technologies like Modelica (for component-oriented systems modelling and simulation) and Autosar (standard for automotive embedded software). 2) Defining interfaces to enable co-simulation among virtual product models and 3) Delivering an integrated process for embedded systems and software.

The above figure depicted the co-simulation to integrate engine, gearbox, thermal system and other automotive divisions. Modelisar functions are majorly benefits to automotive industry. Indeed the workflow between Modelica (systems modelling) and AUTOSAR (embedded software generation) is integrated but the co-simulation is limited to embedded system and software. [Modelisar-08] [ITEA2-12] [Modelisar-11]

ICOS

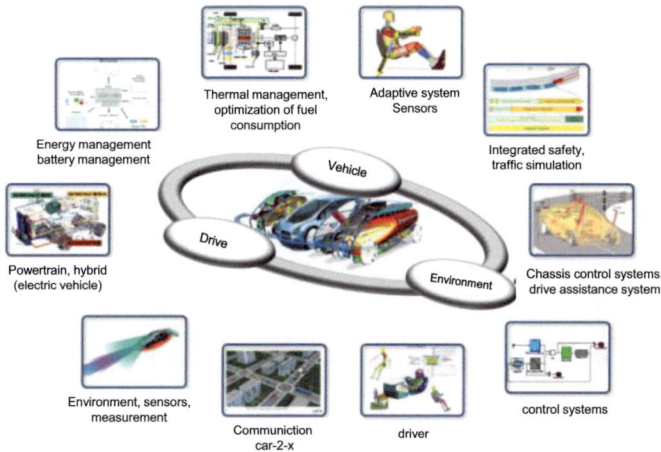

Figure 2. 25 ICOS - a co-simulation platforms

Independent Co-Simulation (ICOS) is developed at Virtual Vehicle. Virtual Vehicle is an international research center for full vehicle system optimization that combines simulation and testing.

The Virtual Vehicle has adapted coupling algorithms (such as Waveform Relaxation or Multi-Rate approach), which are used in "Independent Co-Simulation"-Platform (ICOS). Different simulations have different time constants and when they are coupled without small time-steps it results in error. This error is because physically existing coupling of models is not correctly taken into account when can lead to divergence in co-simulation.

The design of serial hybrid electrical vehicles with a Lithium-Ion battery clearly demonstrates the need for a cross-domain co-simulation (Figure

2.26). Other examples are integrated safety (coupling of FEM crash simulation with vehicle dynamics simulation and controller development), Battery simulation (coupling of electrochemical & thermal models) and thermal simulation (coupling of thermal, electrical and mechanical models for energy management systems).

The validation of several implementation approaches at early stage of development supports the concept; thus reducing development time and cost. Simplified parts with less maturity can be integrated and cosimulated but with parts with high maturity or granularity, it's still an open point to co-simulate. [ZeJo-12]

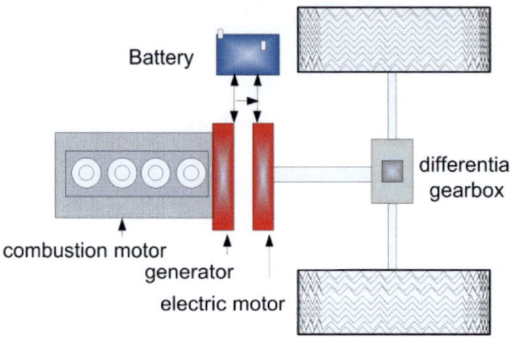

Figure 2. 26 – Design and validation of hybrid electric vehicle

COREPRO

COREPRO project (funded by Uni-Ulm and Daimler AG), elaborates the fundamental requirements for IT support of development processes. In particular, every subcomponent of product has related processes that have to be mapped to overall development process structure and to be synchronized according to the dependencies between subcomponents.

COREPRO is to utilize this information in order to enable automated coordination data driven (i.e., product-driven) process structures. The research work is to support full process life cycle comprising modeling, enactment and change of process structure. It also links products with respect to its dependencies [MuDo-09] [MuRe-08] [BeHe-05]

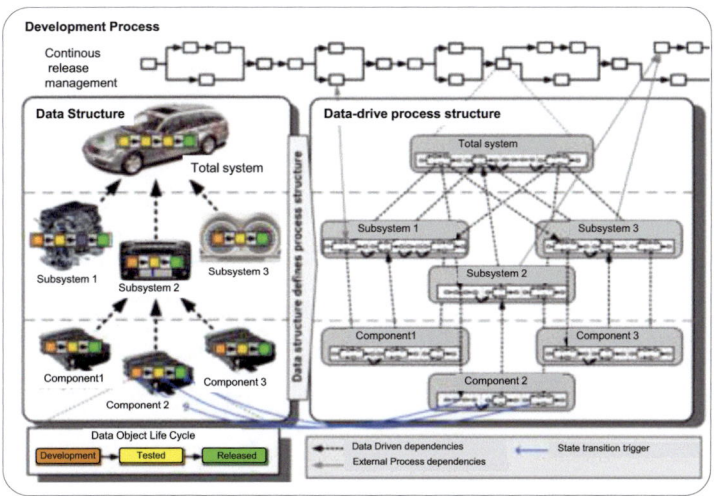

Figure 2. 27 COREPRO Development Process

UWE GÜHL

Dissertation by **Uwe Gühl** on "Design and realization of a modular architecture for a vehicle draft system". It is shown that, especially in early stage of car development, there is possibility to create rapidly car concepts using a modeling tool and to validate these models using simulation tools. In order to address these issues a modular architecture concept is introduced to integrate simulation programs. In a connected relational database the car concept data and configuration data are managed. The project focus was on early stages of car development process and on the function of the product. [GuUw-01]

1 - Feature accomplished 2 - Feature partly accomplished 3 - Feature basically accomplished 4 - Feature not accomplished 0 - Not relevant		Feasibility to identify CAE interdepend-encies	Feasibility to handle comprehensi ve CAE complexity	Feasibility to adapt and customize dependencies	Feasibility to improve traceability and transparency of CAE system	Feasibility to improve accuracy of CAE results	Feasibility to support reduction of hardware prototype
State of Art - Scientific							
	Autosim	4	3	4	3	4	4
CAE Network	Modelisar	3	3	2	2	2	3
	ICOS	4	3	2	2	2	2
	COREPO	3	0	2	0	0	0
	Uwe	3	0	3	2	3	2

Table 2. 4 Evaluation of Scientific - CAE Network

2.3.2 CAE Process

FORFLOW

Simulations are integrated throughout development process. Simulation data quality must be pre-defined with respect to both comprehensiveness and certainty. It is closely connected to a progress of process. Therefore, concerning simulations planning requires a detailed process model.

For this purpose, the model developed by FORFLOW (Bavarian research alliance consisting of six institutes of mechanical engineering and applied informatics of four Bavarian universities) may serve as a basis. The process model has been developed in detailed and variable.

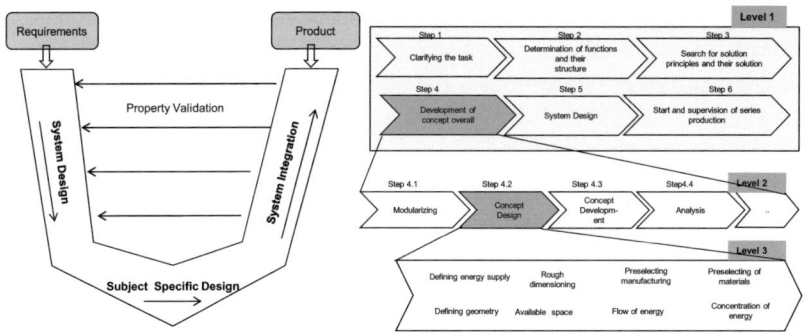

Figure 2. 28 Comparing V-Model and Forflow model

V-Model VDI 2206	FORFLOW Process Model
Strategic process model	Strategic process model
Development process is dissolved in a rough granularity	Framework that provides a sufficient detailing
It is inapplicable for an operative support of product development process	Also allows enough space for its operative arrangement
It pointed out the importance of simulation and integrated it in development process	It relieves the integration of aspects of simulation planning

Table 2. 5 Comparing V-Model and Forflow model

The core objective was to provide optimum process and workflow support to the developer in order to make procedures in the product development process more effective and efficient. The Forflow process model is step forward in detailing than V-Model VDI 2206. The differences between V-Model and Forflow process model are given below.

Simulation planning is necessary to ensure product functionality throughout the development process. The FORFLOW process model provides a framework which is detailed enough to assign questions of simulation planning to the development process more efficiently. In order to make it possible to develop simulation planning approaches, further research activities are being conducted which focus on the organization and optimization of data flows.

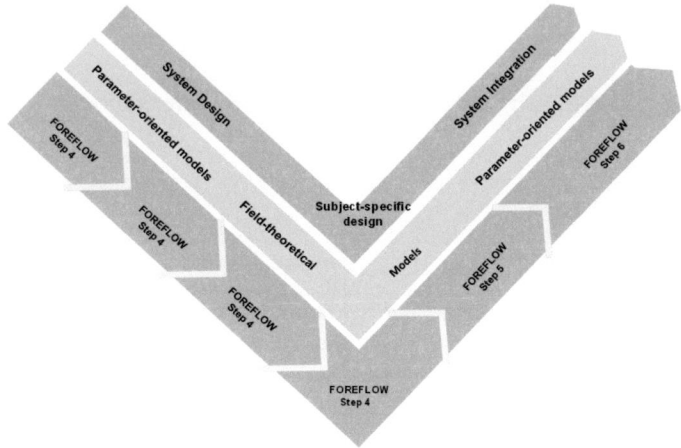

Figure 2. 29 Simulation methods integrated into process methods

T-Systems' proposal for CAE process:

There are various ways to integrate metadata in CAE process. It can be accomplished by improving Pre-processor data which leads to a new FE model definition. The integration of the CAD data is performed including the geometry and metadata of the parts. For preprocessing the parts can be organized like the tree structure. Each Part contains geometry, FE mesh, properties, sets, materials and metadata. All these information aids to build a CAE Process with its dependencies. External references can also be added: [MaSa-09] [KrMa-02]

The state of high-performance computer (HPC) usage in CAE domain proposes an architectural approach to integrate data and processes in simulation data management or PLM environment.

The implementation of HPC has increased in industrial environments and enables a widespread multidisciplinary use for CAE applications. CAE processes are mapped for individual process steps as well as incoming and outgoing information in SADT diagrams. [AnYa-07]

SIMDAT

SIMDAT project was funded by European Commission under Information Society Technologies (IST) for the duration for 48 months. It was started in Sept 20014. The focus of this project was to build data grids for process and product development using numerical simulation and knowledge discovery. Grid technology is used in this project to connect diverse data sources, to enable flexible, and develop refined collaboration.

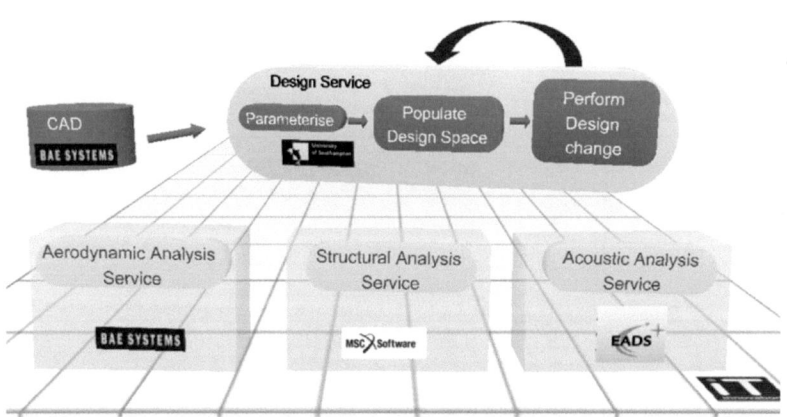

Figure 2. 30 SIMDAt Aero Prototype

An aerospace application is a used as a use-case to simulate multidisciplinary collaborative and building a CAE Process as shown in figure 2.30. The scenario is typical of sub-system design problems in the context of future-concept, unmanned cargo vehicles that require an ability to use airfields in noise-sensitive locations. An inter-enterprise Grid has been deployed between four sites: BAE Systems, EADS, MSC and Southampton University with secure and controlled provisioning of CAE services and workflows. [SIMD-06] [SIMDAT-12]

Major objectives SIMDAT are 1) to test and enhance Grid data technology for product development and production process design. 2) To develop data Grids as a basis for distributed knowledge discover. 3) Verifying seamless data access as a key result of Grid technologies and 4) to raise awareness of advantages of Data Grids.

Key technological layers have been identified as important to SIMDAT.

- an integrated Grid system, with basic services and higher-level process.

- Improve transparency of data repositories

- management of Virtual Organisations and

- scientific workflow

1 - Feature accomplished 2 - Feature partly accomplished 3 - Feature basically accomplished 4 - Feature not accomplished 0 - Not relevant		Feasibility to identify CAE interdepend-encies	Feasibility to handle comprehensive CAE complexity	Feasibility to adapt and customize dependencies	Feasibility to improve traceability and transparency of CAE system	Feasibility to improve accuracy of CAE results	Feasibility to support reduction of hardware prototype
State of Art - Scientific							
CAE Process	V-Model	0	2	3	2	0	0
	ForFlow	0	2	2	2	0	0
	T-System	0	3	4	2	0	0
	SIMDAT	0	2	2	2	0	0

Table 2. 6 Evaluation Scietific - CAE Process

2.3.3 CAE Data Management

A continuous development in Automotive CAE Integration is going on at ProSTEP iViP/VDA. SimPDM project (under ProSTEP iViP/VDA) was started at 2008 with the objective to develop solutions for the integration of simulation and computation in a PDM environment. The first version of the SimPDM recommendation has been published as PSI4 in 2008. Outlook of simPDM were focused in Project "Collaborative CAD/CAE Integration (C3I)". C3I project ended in 2011 and CAE Services is the successor project of C3I. Thereby, the continuous development of CAE Integration has been done by ProSTEP iViP/VDA. Key results of SimPDM, C3I and CAE Services are described in this session.

SimPDM The objective of SimPDM project group is to develop solutions for the integration of simulation and computation in a PDM. The solutions and concepts developed in the project group are to create an integrated development environment in which computation, processes and structures are stored in PDM.

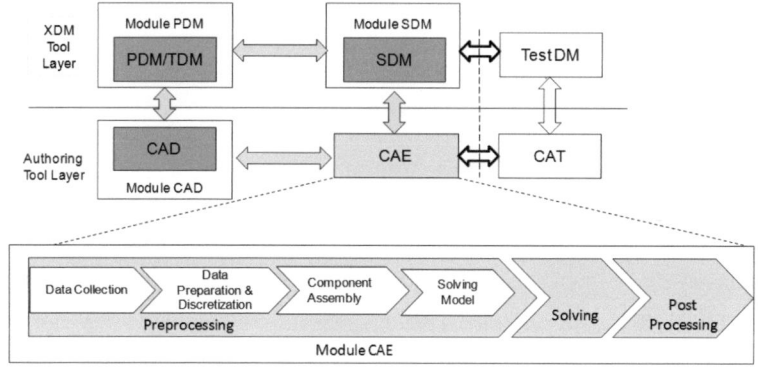

Figure 2. 31 Big Picture of CAD/CAE Integration

SimPDM recommendation constituted an important milestone in the development of simulation data management. However, development execution is not a complete part of the project. SimPDM has been developed further with view to providing better support for a variety of simulation disciplines. This includes both the integration capabilities offered by the SimPDM approach and the functional scope covered by SimPDM.

Collaborative CAD/CAE Integration (C3I) – Automotive CAE Integration – Requirement and Evaluation of Interfaces is done with a contribution of the working group "CAD/CAE Integration" at the steering committee together with 6 German Automotive companies (like Audi, Daimler, Porsche, BMW, VW) under C3I project (figure 2.31)

SDM tool at that time were still in under evaluation. SDM often takes on the role of a TDM for the CAE department underneath a master PDM system, and combines the two basic functionalities data management and workflow master (application process control).
In this SDM module, it is divided into three major divisions (see Picture – Big Picture of Simulation Data Management). 1) Administration, 2) Data Management and 3) Workflow Management / Process Control

SDM Modules in the Administration Layer:

- Long Term Storage: The storage tenure has to be defined for each informative data. The function is to provide an interface to store document in an external archive. Inputs and Outputs of the CAE modules have to be provided.

- Integration of external Partners: The major function to provide SDM access for external partners, data transfer, ability to remotely control simulation runs and interfaces to an external data SimPDM tool.

- Rights and Roles: The function is to create user groups, manage access for functions and data objects through dedicated attributes and life cycle status.

- Lifecycle management: the main task is the definition of status net-works. That means at which stage a CAE data object can have, and the rules which apply for changing the lifecycle stages. So the status information and status network are the main functions.

SDM Modules in the Data Management Layer:

- PDM Base functions – Template Management: Data which are being re-used in a number of simulation runs are automated by templates. Managing the CAE templates, libraries, predefined simulations, load cases, boundaries condition etc are the functions of template management.

- PDM Base functions CAE structure mapping: The structure mapping is to map CAD and CAE structure.

- PDM Base functions – Model Management: it is related to the handling of all kind of CAE models and components.

- PDM Base functions – Model Assembly: To combine and decomposition of sub-models, templates, load cases, setting etc.

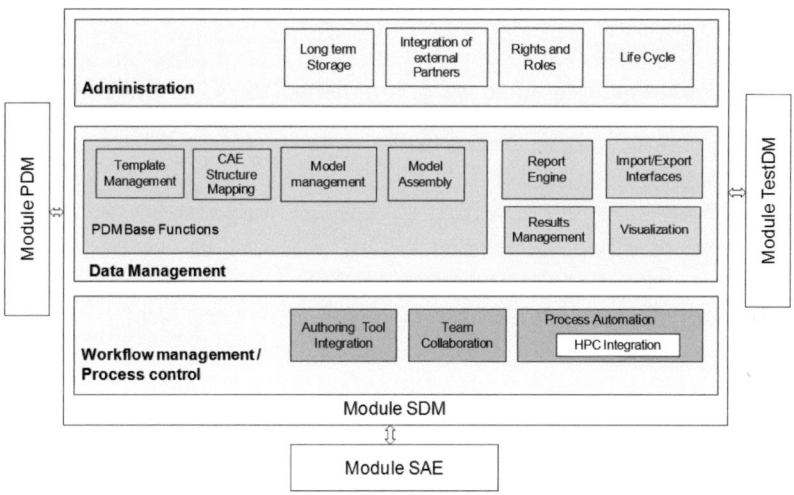

Figure 2 32 Big Picture of Simulation Data Management

- Report Engine: Creation and management of report, graphs, diagrams etc.

- Result Management: Organizing, storage, retrieval and access to simulation results and meta data. Version of results and managing simulation end results to save for longer term.

- Import and Export Interfaces: Management of exchange volumes. Importing and exporting files via interfaces.

- Visualization: CAD and CAE model data visualization. Process visualization is not the focus in this sub-module.

SDM Modules in the Data Management Layer:

- Authoring tool Integration: Access to data management by the SDM from within an authoring tool.

- Team collaboration: Defining, executing and logging of processes in a traceable manner. Management of process templates and visualizing the process flow are the major functions of team collaboration.

- Process Automation: By batch mode, repetitive and re/use data can be automated using commercial tools like simManager.

In this research work, partial implementation in workflow management, automation, visualization is carried out by various software developers. The challenge is to harmonize all modules and to implement. The point to network various simulation ie CAE Network can be highlighted in team collaboration but mapping of CAE results are not yet defined These challenges are highlighted in CAE Services project.

CAE Services is the successor project of the ProSTEP iViP / VDA Project „Collaborative CAD/CAE Integration (C3I)". In C3I the SimPDM results were enhanced by addressing aspects of cross-domain and cross-enterprise CAE processes, giving due consideration to existing standards. The objective of CAE Services is to prepare concrete implementation of solutions and setting up a subsequent C3I Implementer Forum. [KuSh-12] [FaBe-10] [Keln-10] [JeBr-07] [BaBo-10] [BaBo-09] [SimPDM-08].

1 - Feature accomplished 2 - Feature partly accomplished 3 - Feature basically accomplished 4 - Feature not accomplished 0 - Not relevant	Feasibility to identify CAE interdepend-encies	Feasibility to handle comprehensive CAE complexity	Feasibility to adapt and customize dependencies	Feasibility to improve traceability and transparency of CAE system	Feasibility to improve accuracy of CAE results	Feasibility to support reduction of hardware prototype
State of Art - Scientific						
CAE Data Management SimPDM	3	3	4	2	0	0
C3I	2	2	2	1	0	0
CAE Services	2	2	1	1	0	0

Table 2. 7 Evaluation of Scientific - Simulation Data Management

2.4 Chapter Summary

The Chapter State of art encloses various methods and tools from industries as well as science. Evaluation results are collected in Table 2.8 and improvement areas are highlighted in grey.

Summarizing the outcome of state of art as per the features is as follows:

- Identifying CAE interdependencies: Being a key feature for networking and sharing the information among CAE system, it has to be the prime requirement. However, this feature is not accomplished in any of method or tool. As given in table 2.8, features to identify CAE interdependencies required most attention. In some commercial tools like SimManager and Team Centre, it is introduced as basic feature. User has to define the dependency and manually selecting the dependent simulation. Thus, **extracting interdependencies among simulations to build a CAE Network is a principal requirement of this research**.

- Handling comprehensive CAE complexity: building a method for diverse and vast CAE system is a bottleneck of any CAE methodology. Indeed SimPDM, C3I and CAE-Services research projects and their results are well equipped with this feature but implementing brings new challenges. Thereby, extension of

1 - Feature accomplished 2 - Feature partly accomplished 3 - Feature basically accomplished 4 - Feature not accomplished 0 - Not relevant		Feasibility to identify CAE interdependencies	Feasibility to handle comprehensive CAE complexity	Feasibility to adapt and customize dependencies	Feasibility to improve traceability and transparency of CAE	Feasibility to improve accuracy of CAE results	Feasibility to support hardware reduction of prototype
State of Art - Industrial							
CAE Network	Daimler	4	2	4	3	2	2
	Audi	4	2	3	2	2	3
	BMW	4	2	4	2	2	3
	GM-Opel	4	3	3	4	3	3
	Toyota	4	3	4	3	2	3
CAE Process	Daimler	0	3	3	3	0	0
	Audi	0	1	2	2	0	0
	BMW	0	1	2	2	0	0
	GM-Opel	0	2	3	2	0	0
	Toyota	0	3	3	2	0	0
CAE Data Management	Daimler	3	4	4	2	0	0
	Audi	3	2	3	1	0	0
	BMW	3	2	3	1	0	0
	GM-Opel	4	4	4	4	0	0
	Toyota	4	4	4	4	0	0
State of Art - Scientific							
CAE Network	Autosim	4	3	4	3	4	4
	Modelisar	3	3	2	2	2	3
	ICOS	4	3	2	2	2	2
	COREPO	3	0	2	0	0	0
	Uwe	3	0	3	2	3	2
CAE Process	V-Model	0	2	3	2	0	0
	ForFlow	0	2	2	2	0	0
	T-System	0	3	4	2	0	0
	SIMDAT	0	2	2	2	0	0
CAE Data Management	SimPDM	3	3	4	2	0	0
	C3I	2	2	2	1	0	0
	CAE Services	2	2	1	1	0	0

Table 2. 8 Evaluation results - State of Art

existing methods can be done by analyzing the system failures.

- Adapting and customizing dependencies: Within phases of vehicle development process the dependency varies as maturity of a product increases. Dependencies also depend of type of product and priority of product. Therefore, **extracting dependencies and adapting it as per product and phases is a foremost requirement in automotive industry**. In CAE Network, this feature is partly accomplished however it applies for individual simulation.

- Traceability and transparency of CAE System: Although all CAE Network, CAE Process and CAE data management aims to improve traceability and transparency of CAE System. Still this feature is available at basic level in commercial tools. The traceability and transparency of CAD data is at mature level but CAE processes are still at static level. **This leads to a new requirement of optimizing existing processes to collaborate CAE Teams.**

- Improving accuracy of CAE results: Collecting failures due to lack of CAE Network, CAE Process or CAE data management helps in identifying potential of the work. CAE Network by mutiphysics and cosimulation foster accuracy of CAE results. Mapping various simulations is one of the requirements of mutiphysics and integrating mapping features in CAE data management enrich existing methods.

- Supporting in reduction of hardware prototype: Fundamental requirement of CAE is to reduce the hardware prototype. CAE Networks truly aids in support to reduce the hardware prototype. **To enhance reducing the hardware prototype, CAE Network and CAE Process have to be integrated to CAE data management.**

The outcome of this chapter leads to define a methodology which helps to define the objectives of new methods to fill highlighted gaps.

3 A NEW METHODOLOGY- "CAE-ProNet"

Previous chapter "State of Art" describes and evaluates similar methodologies of current systems to network simulations. Using the evaluation results of existing methodologies, a new methodology is developed which is called as CAE-ProNet. The methodology and its detailed description are in this chapter, which is a core of this research work. This chapter includes:

- Objectives of CAE-ProNet methodology (Section 3.1)

- Approach of the methodology (Section 3.2)

- Detail description of the methodology (Section 3.3)

- Added values of the methodology (Section 3.4 and 3.5)

- Summary of this chapter (Section 3.6)

3.1 Methodology Objective

The major objective of CAE-ProNet methodology is to improve quality of simulations by using digital results of dependent simulations as inputs. Simulations and their load cases which are simplified have to compromise with quality as they use less parameter as inputs to carry out computation. CAE-ProNet methodology helps to use detailed and to use actual parameters from another simulation that already exist in the organization or a work group, thus improves the quality of simulation. Another objective is to eliminate hardware based inputs. In this era of 3D virtual engineering, many simulation disciplines are still dependent on hardware prototypes. Generally, hardware prototypes are developed in later phases of development process. Therefore, dependent simulations use assumptions which are constructed on a base of experiences of previous results. The methodology aims to reduce dependency on hardware prototype testing which ultimately results in cost reduction. It opens possibilities to simulate and validate a system in early stages due to independency on hardware results. By the networking of simulations those lead to team collaboration, has a focus to reduce the complexity of entire simulation system. Based on above major factors objectives are constructed as follows.

3.1.1 Objective – System Analysis

The objective is to analyze simulation failures in a system that can be solved. Symptoms of simulation failures and quality reports evaluation helps to figure out the areas of enhancements. System analysis aids to check the sustainability of CAE-ProNet methodology for that particular system and provides support to management decisions to go on implementation of the methodology.

3.1.2 Objective – Extracting Dependencies

One of the objectives of this methodology is to develop a library of generic dependencies among simulations. In current methods, there is no such criterion to identify dependencies among simulations on theoretical bases. The library model is generic and can also be implemented in other industries or organization that applies simulations to validate design of product. The library helps to figure out most of the simulation dependencies, irrespective of product, priority and development phase. Above all, it recognizes each single dependency that is mostly ignored due to minor relevance. Later on identifies dependencies can be customized according to specific requirements.

3.1.3 Objective – Team Collaboration

Customization of generic dependencies for a particular work group is a core functionality of CAE-ProNet methodology. It makes work group's data effectively accessible among all users. Thus, it enables to collaborate various simulation departments, teams and engineers.

Moreover, better structuring of simulation life cycle by visualizing team collaborations is an additional advantage.

3.1.4 Objective – Optimizing Existing Process

A sequence of CAE operations that are planned and executed in accordance with company requirements and policies is known as CAE Process. It involves relevant stakeholders who monitor, control, and evaluates established process. To optimize it with respect to work group requirement is an objective of CAE-ProNet methodology. An algorithm is used to generate and optimize CAE process that also aids in controlling the quality gates.

3.1.5 Objective – Integration to Simulation Data Management

Besides all above objectives, an application is designed and developed that defines actions for each user type and helps to execute the CAE-ProNet methodology. It aims to illustrate necessary functionalities and steps for users to avail the methodology in the best possible way. Additionally it figures out integration possibilities of CAE ProNet Application with Simulation Data Management System.

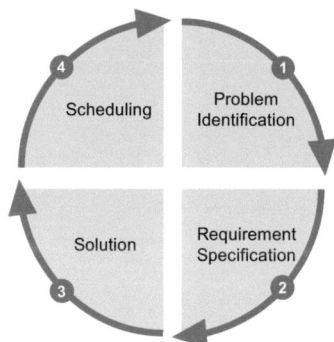

Figure 3. 1 General Structure of CAE-ProNet methodology

3.2 Methodological Approach

An approach to fulfill above objectives of the methodology is described in this section. The general structure of methodology is portrayed in four phase as shown in figure 3.1. Phase-1 starts with "Problem Identification". Problems can be figured by collecting failures of vehicle during digital validation and hardware testing. After analyzing, evaluating and defining the problems in CAE, requirement specifications are described in phase 2.

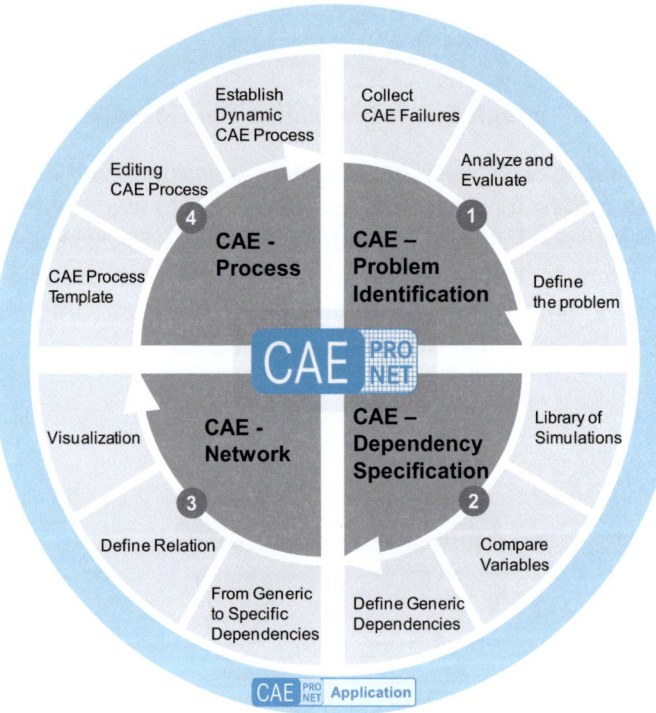

Figure 3. 2 CAE-ProNet methodology

Requirement specifications are compared to theoretical specifications of that particular system which leads to figure the solution in phase 3. At the end in phase 4, the scheduling of the tasks according to the solution is mentioned. After the scheduling and execution of complete loop phase 1 restarts, as it is a continuous closed loop system.

The CAE-ProNet methodology lies in core of the system and the digital solution "CAE-ProNet Application" encircled the system. Top-Right quarter of the inner circle represents the starting point as phase 1 "CAE – Problem Identification" and outer circle represents the steps of phase "CAE – Problem Identification". The continuity goes until Top-Left quarter where the first loop ends and then a new loop starts.

Each phase is divided into further three steps, as demonstrated in figure 3.2. Description of each sub step is given below:

- **Phase 1 "CAE – Problem Identification"**: Phase-1 starts by collecting the failures and feedback of CAE engineers on the existing validation process. For example, the quality reports of durability simulation for car doors have uncertain results. Upon this, feedback of simulation engineers is that they used results of previous vehicles hardware testing results as inputs for latest vehicles. This data is necessary to analyze and evaluate. Focus of evaluations is simulation problems related to interconnected simulations. Finally the problem in CAE system is defined using symptoms, system analysis and evaluation results.

- **Phase 2 "CAE Dependency Specification"**: After phase 1, the dependency specifications are figured out using generic relation among simulations. The generic relations are based on theoretical aspects of the simulations. Equation's variables of each simulation are collected and compared to define a generic relation.

- **Phase 3 "CAE Network"**: From generic to specific relation of simulation are expressed in this phase to build a CAE network of dependencies among simulations. Various relations with different granularity are explained and visualized in this step 3. In broad-spectrum it's a solution of problem identified by specifications of dependencies.

- **Phase 4 "CAE Process":** A dynamic CAE process is established which helps to perform in an optimized way and simultaneously identifies problem in the system to start the next iteration.

The methodology is enclosed with a digital solution called CAE-ProNet application that helps to elaborate the role of users and organization systems. Each phase of CAE-ProNet methodology and major functionalities of CAE-ProNet application are elaborated and described in section 3.3.

3.3 Methodology Description

As described in section 3.2, this section contains detailed description of the methodology. Each phase describes its objectives, steps to implement, example to elaborate, exceptional conditions (method boundaries) and summary. Aerodynamics simulation, stiffness simulation and dependencies between them are used as a general example in this section.

The methodology phases are illustrated in following tables:

Table 3. 1 Phase 1 CAE-Problem Identification

Table 3. 3 Phase 2 CAE-Dependency Specification

Table 3. 4 Phase 3 CAE-Network

Table 3. 5 Phase 4 - CAE-Process

3.3.1 CAE – Problem Identification

Phase-1: CAE- Problem Identification

Introduction

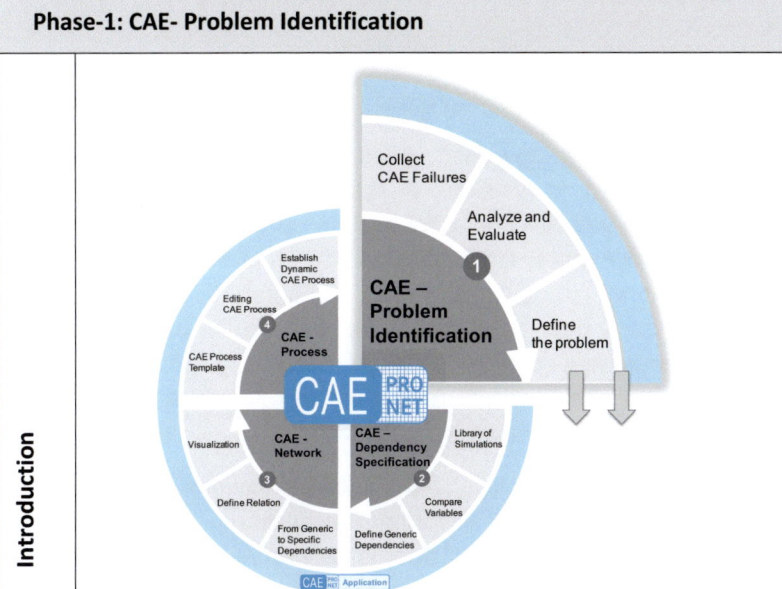

Figure 3. 3 Phase 1 of CAE-ProNet Methodology

CAE-Problem Identification phase analyse and evaluate organization CAE System and identify problems that can be solved using CAE-ProNet methodology. An example is elaborated (Motorhood) in chapter-5 where 35% of load cases are identified as dependent to other load cases. This phase helps managers to take decision for executing CAE-ProNet Methodology.

Objective

Major objectives of phase-1 are to evaluate system sustainability and to define problems in CAE system that can be solved using CAE-ProNet methodology. Symptom are elaborated which helps to identify CAE Problems. Foremost applicability of this methodology is anticipated in the area of manufacturing industry and specific to automotive.

The phase starts from the step collecting CAE-failures, analyze & evaluate and finally defining the problem as shown in fig 3.3.

Step 1 – Collect CAE-Failures:

Collect all simulations, load cases and their descriptions which are performed to validate a system and its products. For example, to validate front door system durability, aerodynamics, structural dynamics, crash simulations are performed. Durability has torsional, buckling and high temperature load cases to validate car's door durability. Collecting the list of simulations, load cases and their description containing pre-processing, solving and post-processing of a system, this is a first step to identify the area of enhancement.

Bring together the quality reports of simulations during digital validation process. For example, the durability requirement for the composite-laminate car door is defined as a condition that a door must endure 1.5×10^9 cycles of torsional loading without failing when subjected to 3-degree torsion. These requirements have to be fulfilled while digital validation. After computational results, quality reports describe failures and errors for that particular system.

Step 2 – Analyze and Evaluate

Analyzing the results and failures on the basis of symptoms as follows:

Symptom-1: **Simplified or assumption based load case:** Collect analysis cases where the inputs are used as simplified load or assumption based on previous results. For example, to validate car's front door stiffness due to wind, n KN of single point force in outer direction is used to validate the design. These inputs know-how are from simulation experts.

(Steps and Example)

Symptom-2: **Hardware Prototype Testing Results**: Results of hardware prototype testing as input of simulations and load cases are another symptom of improvement. Improvement is required as hardware testing can only be done at end of development phase. These hardware testing results can only be used in upcoming versions of system or products.

Thus, the actual data is not used to perform computation. For example, in fatigue simulation it's assumed that: (i) the vehicle at hand has six cylinders; (ii) total mileage = 270000 km; (iii) average vehicle speed=80 km/h; (iv) average engine speed = 2500 rpm. The computation yielded 1.5 billion cycles. These data are from hardware testing and used as inputs for all versions for fatigue analysis.

Symptom-3: **Ignorance of relevant inputs**: This symptom is common in most of the industries. Ignorance of various diminutive inputs results in reduced quality, as it is difficult to calculate including all dependencies.

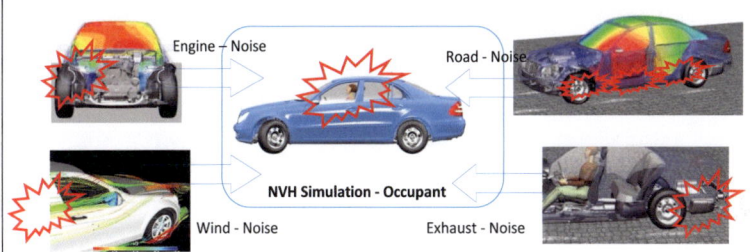

Figure 3. 4 NVH Simulation for Occupant

Steps and Example

Steps and Example

As in figure 3.4, for Noise calculation (NVH Simulation) for occupant various sources have to be considered. Major noise source are engine noise, road noise, wind noise and exhaust noise. Other noise sources are vibration noise, environment noise etc. In practice, we consider only major sources and most of the time NVH simulation are performed for individual source. Indeed the source information exists within organization but difficult to execute. Moreover minor sources are ignored. This results in decreasing the quality of simulation results.

Another example of simulating lifetime of vehicle door's opening mechanism. Pressure inside vehicle, temperature influence, thickness deviations in sheet metal (from manufacturing process) are ignored due to minute influences. These minute factors affect in final validation.

Three major symptoms are highlighted in this research work. Highlighted part is that most of the dependent simulations are under these symptoms. In chapter-5, it is given that for motorhood load cases are 35% dependent. Out of 35% dependent simulations, 85% simulations are under these symptoms.

Later on evaluating symptoms are major tasks. Evaluations can be accomplished using quality reports of specified symptoms of simulations. Simulations experts view plays a major role in evaluating CAE problems that can be solved using the CAE ProNet methodology.

Step 3 – Define the problem:

Finally, evaluation is summarized by defining the simulation and its analysis cases that need modifications.

	List of these simulations helps to take decision on implementing the CAE ProNet methodology.
	This method steps helps to decide the implementation benefits of CAE-ProNet methodology. The identified problem will be sent to phase-2 "CAE dependencies specification" to check its generic dependencies.
Exceptions	There can be numerous problems or failures in CAE. The phase-1 "Problem identification" is focusing on dependencies among simulations and load cases. Failures due to mesh, connections, computational method, or computation tool are not involved. Dependency on electrical, electronics and mechatronic systems are also not in covered in this thesis.
Summary	The summary of step-1 is that user can evaluate their system problem that can be solved using the CAE ProNet methodology. Given symptoms and failure type helps to figure out CAE problems. The phase helps managers to decide whether to go or no-go with the methodology for their organization or work group.

Table 3. 1 Phase 1 CAE-Problem Identification

3.3.2 CAE – Dependency Specification

Phase-2: CAE- Dependency Specification

Introduction	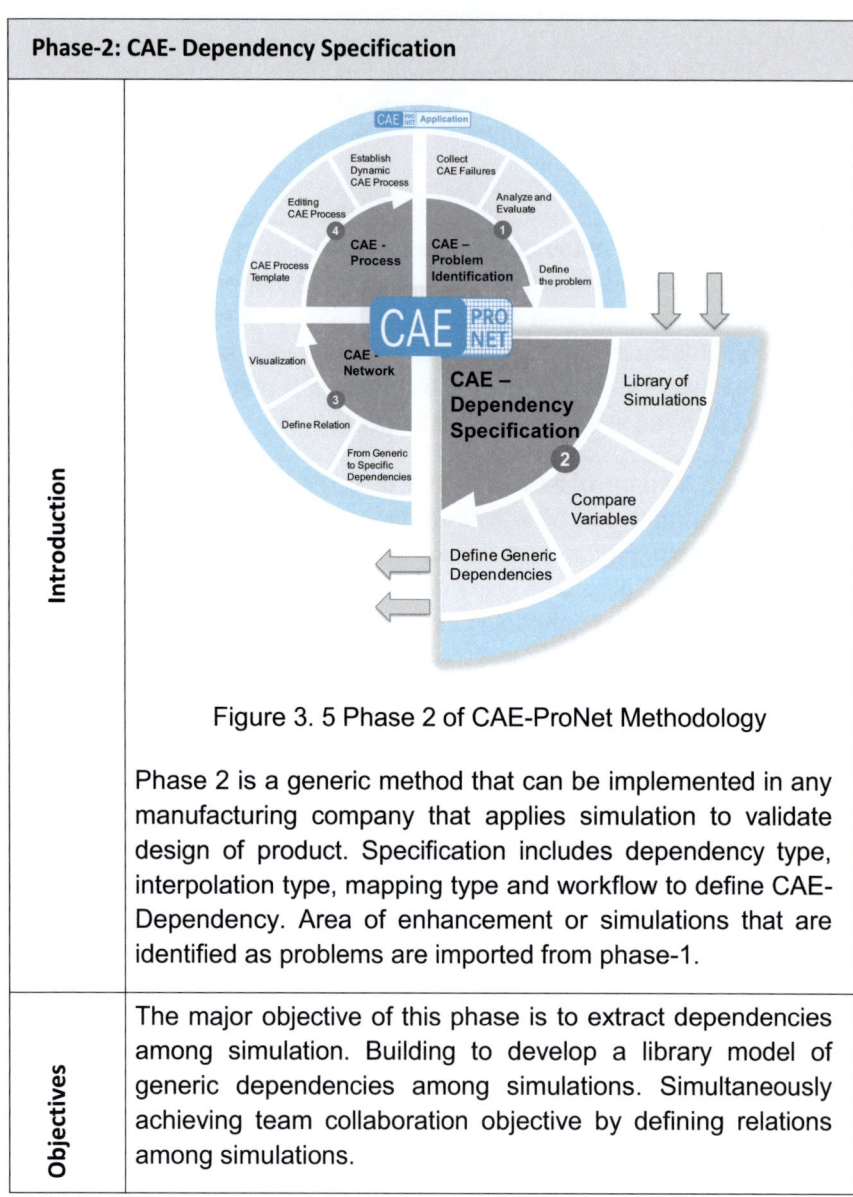 Figure 3. 5 Phase 2 of CAE-ProNet Methodology Phase 2 is a generic method that can be implemented in any manufacturing company that applies simulation to validate design of product. Specification includes dependency type, interpolation type, mapping type and workflow to define CAE-Dependency. Area of enhancement or simulations that are identified as problems are imported from phase-1.
Objectives	The major objective of this phase is to extract dependencies among simulation. Building to develop a library model of generic dependencies among simulations. Simultaneously achieving team collaboration objective by defining relations among simulations.

Stepss

It has 3 steps – library of simulations, comparing variables and finally defining generic relation, as demonstrated in Figure 3.5. These steps are written in cook book format to simplify the explanation of each step.

Step-1 Library of simulations:

- Prepare a set *"S"* which contains *n* number of simulations that are particularly used in any organization those are used to validate product design.
- List theoretical equ. for each of simulation in Set "S".
- List all the parameters involved in those equations to construct a table as shown in table 3.2. The table can be generated for any simulation and its equations that involve inputs, outputs or actors as variables. Furthermore, it may also involve constants that can be universal or specific parameter of that simulation. (Variables are of 3 types Input, Output and Actor). There are many theories and scientific ways to perform aerodynamics simulations. Navier-Strokes, Euler, Bernoulli equations are some example. Key factor is that basic parameters of all equations are same as explain below.

$$\begin{cases} \dfrac{\partial u}{\partial x} + \dfrac{\partial v}{\partial y} = 0 \\ -\dfrac{\partial P}{\partial x} = \rho.V_x.\dfrac{\partial V_x}{\partial x} + \rho.V_y.\dfrac{\partial V_x}{\partial y} - \mu.\dfrac{\partial^2 V_x}{\partial x^2} - \mu.\dfrac{\partial^2 V_x}{\partial y^2} + \rho.\dfrac{\partial V_x}{\partial t} - \rho.g_x \\ -\dfrac{\partial P}{\partial y} = \rho.V_x.\dfrac{\partial V_y}{\partial x} + \rho.V_y.\dfrac{\partial V_y}{\partial y} - \mu.\dfrac{\partial^2 V_y}{\partial x^2} - \mu.\dfrac{\partial^2 V_y}{\partial y^2} + \rho.\dfrac{\partial V_y}{\partial t} - \rho.g_y \end{cases}$$

- Repeat above steps for the remaining simulation from Set *"S"*.

Steps

Euler (in viscid compressible fluid) [MIT-05] [BoBa-02] [NaJa-99]

$$
\begin{cases}
\dfrac{\partial \rho}{\partial t} + \dfrac{\partial(\rho.V_x)}{\partial x} + \dfrac{\partial(\rho.V_y)}{\partial y} = 0 \\[2ex]
\dfrac{\partial(\rho.V_x)}{\partial t} + \dfrac{\partial(P+\rho.V_x^2)}{\partial x} + \dfrac{\partial(\rho.V_x.V_y)}{\partial y} = 0 \\[2ex]
\dfrac{\partial(\rho.V_y)}{\partial t} + \dfrac{\partial(\rho.V_x.V_y)}{\partial x} + \dfrac{\partial(P+\rho.V_y^2)}{\partial y} = 0 \\[2ex]
\dfrac{\partial E}{\partial t} + \dfrac{\partial(V_x.(E+P))}{\partial x} + \dfrac{\partial(V_y.(E+P))}{\partial y} = 0
\end{cases}
$$

Bernoulli (inviscid compressible fluid). [Jank-00] [Barn-79] [Smit-92] [Weig-04] [Kim-09]

$$
\frac{1}{2}.\left(V_x^2 + V_y^2\right) + g_y.y + \left(\frac{\gamma}{\gamma-1}\right).\frac{P}{\rho} = cst
$$

All above aerodynamics equations have common parameters like. P - Pressure , V_x V_y – velocity in specific direction, ρ – density of fluid, μ – viscosity of fluid and g_x g_y – gravitational acceleration in specific direction. All are accumulated in table 3.2

	Variables			Constants	
	Input	Output	Actor	Univ.	Spec.
P		x			
Vx	x				
Vy	x				
ρ			x		
µ			x		
gx				x	
gy				x	
E					x
e					x

Table 3. 2 Parameters of Navier-Stroke Equation

Step -2 Compare Variables:

Take simulation x from above mentioned set *"S"* and choose simulation y (other than simulation x) in order to define the relation. E.g. Simulation x is Aerodynamics simulation which is performed using Naviers-Stroke Equation and Simulation y is Stiffness simulation which is performed by Hooke's equation.

- Find out if a mapping is needed for the dependent simulation. If yes then which type of mapping. E.g. Mapping is required for dependency between aerodynamic simulation and stiffness analysis as aerodynamic simulation is performed with environment mesh (Source mesh as in figure 3.6), and stiffness analysis is performed with product or element mesh (Target mesh as in figure 3.6). There are various interpolation method used for mapping process. Examples are linear, polynomial and nearest interpolation method. n.

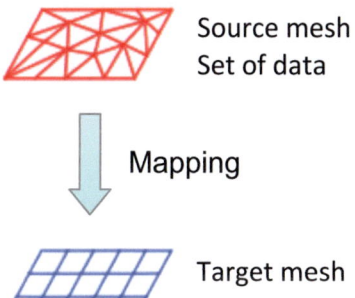

Source mesh
Set of data

Mapping

Target mesh

Figure 3. 6 Mapping from source to target mesh

- Analyze the library of simulation by comparing the input(s) and output(s) parameters of simulations.

Steps

Steps

If the output of one simulation is same as an input for other, than it states a theoretic dependency. This step is fundamental to extract dependencies among simulations to build a library

Step -3 Define Generic Relation:

- After that, figure out which kind of dependency exists among simulations. It can be parameter, material or/and model. The type of dependency exists between two simulations can be generic or specific to CAE strategy of the organization. A) A parametric dependency is generic as it's based on theory, as presented in the previous step. B) A dependency on material is a practical dependency: it is not an output from simulation calculations, but an output from the simulation results. It is a decision by engineers who specifies a new material. C) Model dependency is the most common dependency as same FE-model is used by various simulation engineers.

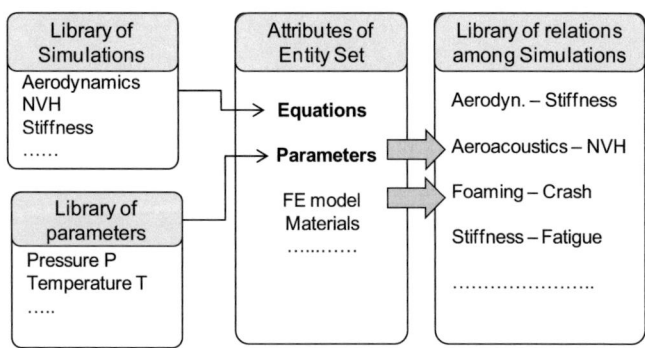

Figure 3. 7 Process to develop library among simulations

- Repeat the process to specify more dependencies and mapping. Finally, all the common parameters are analyzed to define the generic dependencies or relation.

Example	A detailed example of dependency and its specification between stiffness and aerodynamics is explained as follows.

Aerodynamics is the study of the motion of air interacting with a moving object. In automotive industry, it aims at reducing as much as possible the force (or pressure) due to the wind flows around the car.

The equation used for Aerodynamic simulation in commercial tools varies according to the need of application. The basic equation used for aerodynamics is Naviers-Stroke Equation. The following Naviers-Stokes equation (incompressible viscous fluid) concern a 2 dimensional problem (XY plane).

Naviers-Stokes equation (incompressible viscous fluid, 2D), Euler equation (inviscid compressible fluid, 2D) and Bernoulli's equations are accumulated as explained in above steps.

The **parameters** are: P the pressure, Vx the velocity in x-direction, Vy the velocity in y-direction ρ the density of the fluid μ the viscosity of the fluid gx the gravitational acceleration in x-direction, gy the gravitational acceleration in y-direction E the total energy per unit volume, e being the internal energy per unit mass For digital Aerodynamic simulation, an initial velocity input is applied. In addition, reference pressure and density (and often temperature) are given to specify the initial state of the fluid. The main output is pressure distribution (in static) after steady state is reached. As the pressure distribution is obtained depending on evolution of fluid density and speed (and sometimes temp.e), these parameters can also be studied as outputs.

Stiffness Analysis is the study of strain of materials reacting to an applied stress. The displacement and deformation of products due to internal and external load cases are analyzed. |

Stiffness analysis can be performed using reference geometries formulas But in practice, the structure geometries are too complex; thus finite element method is used. The stress-strain relation is calculated for each element of the structure, and the matrices are assembled for a complete solution of the structure.

Following Major theories used to calculate solve stiffness are Hooke' law, theory of plates & shell and theory of Beams. Simplified equation of each theory in given below.

Hooke's law [CHI-07] [ShAr-91] [Wald-96]

$$
\begin{Bmatrix} \sigma_{xx} \\ \sigma_{yy} \\ \sigma_{zz} \\ \sigma_{yz} \\ \sigma_{zx} \\ \sigma_{xy} \end{Bmatrix} = \frac{E}{(1+\upsilon)(1-2\upsilon)} \begin{bmatrix} 1-\upsilon & \upsilon & \upsilon & 0 & 0 & 0 \\ \upsilon & 1-\upsilon & \upsilon & 0 & 0 & 0 \\ \upsilon & \upsilon & 1-\upsilon & 0 & 0 & 0 \\ 0 & 0 & 0 & \frac{1-2\upsilon}{2} & 0 & 0 \\ 0 & 0 & 0 & 0 & \frac{1-2\upsilon}{2} & 0 \\ 0 & 0 & 0 & 0 & 0 & \frac{1-2\upsilon}{2} \end{bmatrix} \begin{Bmatrix} \varepsilon_{xx} \\ \varepsilon_{yy} \\ \varepsilon_{zz} \\ \varepsilon_{yz} \\ \varepsilon_{zx} \\ \varepsilon_{xy} \end{Bmatrix} - \frac{E\alpha T}{1-2\upsilon} \begin{Bmatrix} 1 \\ 1 \\ 1 \\ 0 \\ 0 \\ 0 \end{Bmatrix}
$$

Theory of plates and shells [NiSt-07] [VeKr-01]

$$
\begin{Bmatrix} \sigma_{xx} \\ \sigma_{yy} \\ \sigma_{zz} \end{Bmatrix} = \frac{E}{1-\upsilon^2} \cdot \begin{bmatrix} 1 & \upsilon & 0 \\ \upsilon & 1 & 0 \\ 0 & 0 & \frac{1-\upsilon}{2} \end{bmatrix} \cdot \begin{Bmatrix} \varepsilon_{xx} \\ \varepsilon_{yy} \\ \gamma_{xy} \end{Bmatrix}
$$

Theory of Beams [Nish-11] [SaGh-11]

Example

$$
\begin{Bmatrix} \sigma_{xx} \\ \sigma_{yy} \\ \sigma_{zz} \\ \sigma_{yz} \\ \sigma_{zx} \\ \sigma_{xy} \end{Bmatrix} =
\begin{bmatrix}
\dfrac{EA}{l} & & & & & \\[2mm]
0 & \dfrac{12EI_z}{l^3(1+\Phi_y)} & & \text{Symmetric} & & \\[3mm]
0 & \dfrac{6EI_z}{l^2(1+\Phi_y)} & \dfrac{(4+\Phi_y)EI_z}{l(1+\Phi_y)} & & & \\[3mm]
\dfrac{-EA}{l} & 0 & 0 & \dfrac{EA}{l} & & \\[3mm]
0 & \dfrac{-12EI_z}{l^3(1+\Phi_y)} & \dfrac{-6EI_z}{l^2(1+\Phi_y)} & 0 & \dfrac{12EI_z}{l^3(1+\Phi_y)} & \\[3mm]
0 & \dfrac{6EI_z}{l^2(1+\Phi_y)} & \dfrac{(2-\Phi_y)EI_z}{l(1+\Phi_y)} & 0 & \dfrac{6EI_z}{l^2(1+\Phi_y)} & \dfrac{(4+\Phi_y)EI_z}{l(1+\Phi_y)}
\end{bmatrix}
\begin{Bmatrix} \varepsilon_{xx} \\ \varepsilon_{yy} \\ \varepsilon_{zz} \\ \varepsilon_{yz} \\ \varepsilon_{zx} \\ \varepsilon_{xy} \end{Bmatrix}
$$

The **parameters** of the following equations are:[σ] the stress tensor [ε] the deformation tensor, v the Poisson's coefficient, E the Young's modulus, G the shear modulus, ρ the density of the material ,A the section area of the beam, Iz the second moment of area of the beam, I the length of the beam α the coefficient of thermal expansion, and T the temperature For digital Stiffness simulation, load cases are applied. They can be punctual forces (in N), torques (in N.m), distributed pressure (in N.m2) or a combination of these load cases. Consequently, the input parameter is a force or a pressure (or both). Also, the material properties of the FEA model are provided: density, Young's modulus, Poisson's ratio, shears modulus, etc. The output of Stiffness simulation is the displacement (or strain) of the structure.

Dependency between Aerodynamic and Stiffness simulations is both dependency on model and data. First, geometry of the structure has to be the same for both validation methods (dependency on model), even if the. Aerodynamic simulation only needs the geometry of the outer surface to study the forces caused by the fluid.

Example

On the other hand, there is a data dependency – "Pressure". "Pressure distribution" as out of aerodynamic simulation is used as inputs for Stiffness simulation.

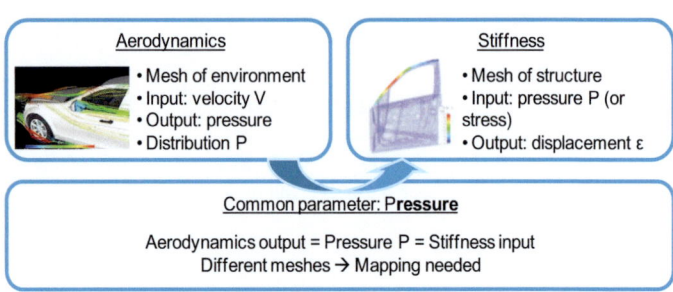

Figure 3. 8 Dependency between Aerodynamics and Stiffness

In practice, some exceptional scenarios have to be considered. In such cases, the library of dependencies can be modified manually in order to rectify mistakes to create new dependency.

Exception-1 Spatial boundaries:

While defining an equation, the field of application is also specified. For instance, a stiffness calculation has to be performed on a structural model, while an aerodynamic simulation cannot be performed on a structural model. The properties of the equations are not valid if the criteria are not respected. For two simulations, if simulation-1 results in an output parameter p that is common with the input parameter of simulation-2, a dependency will be defined between both simulations.

Exceptions

If the spatial field of application of simulation-1 is different from the spatial field of simulation-2 (no common boundary), the method declares a dependency anyway which does not exist in real.

In the example shown in Figure 3.9, the motor cylinder system with Piston is composed of two fields: the environment (air) on the left (Field 1) and the structure on the right (Field 2).

On the other side, we know that simulation-2 (calculated only on Field 2) needs the parameter "pressure" as an input. Then, the output of simulation-1 is the same as the input of simulation-2. Consequently, there is, theoretically, a dependency from simulation-1 to simulation-2.

But, as the fields of applications are different, this pressure does not represent the same physical parameter: in simulation-1, this parameter concerns Field 1, and only Field 1. In simulation-2, this parameter concerns Field 2, and only Field 2: the input pressure comes from another simulation, for example the Multibody Simulation of the system.

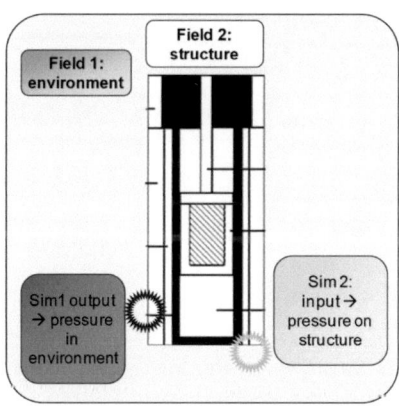

Figure 3. 9 Exception - Spatial Boundaries

This specificity leads to the definition of a dependency that should not be defined. As the method is generic, and as the dependency between simulations also depends on load case, the library of dependencies can be modified manually to meet the requirements of an organization

Exception-2 Non Existence of Parameter in standard equations:

The behavior of a system is governed by equations, but can also be governed by isolated parameters. These parameters can come indirectly from other simulations, but are not always considered as outputs. In this case, the dependency is not defined, even if it exists

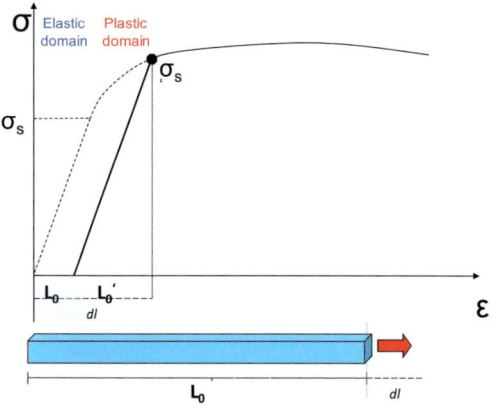

Figure 3. 10 Exception - Non Existance of Standardized Parameter

During forming simulation, properties of material are modified as well as geometry of the system. Among these properties, yield strength is modified, but not considered as an output because it's not calculated during forming simulation. After the traction of a beam, its length and yield strength are increased as shown in figure 3.10

The yield strength (as well as the part's geometry) is relevant for the crash simulation. As the yield strength is not an output of the forming simulation, this modified parameter is not suggested as input for the crash simulation. And yet, in theory, there is a significant dependency because of these parameters. [StFl-04] [Royl-00] [DiKo-97]

In order to overcome this situation, such a dependency can be added manually in the library of dependencies

Exception-3 Manual editing of material properties or/and parameters:

Simulations are governed by equations and an equation is composed of at least one parameter. The exception occurred when an engineer changes a parameter manually. For example, the stiffness simulation uses the stress as main input, and the strain as main output. But other parameters are given to perform the simulation, like properties of structure's material.

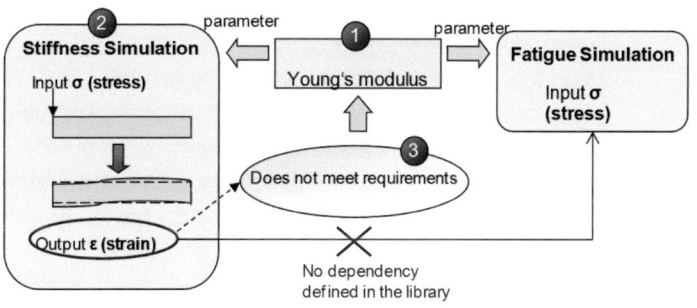

Figure 3. 11 Exception - Manual Editing of material Parameter

The Young's modulus is an explicit example of the scenario: its value is set at the beginning of calculation and does not change during simulation (considered as a constant). But if the simulation's results are not satisfying, engineer can decide to specify other material properties for the structure, and to change young's modulus value. In this case, the young's modulus is not an explicit output of the simulation. But it is an output of the whole simulation. This value can be used as an input for fatigue simulation (for instance). But the dependency does not appear in the library: it has to be added manually.

Exception-4 Material and Model Dependency Type

Additionally to the dependencies on parameters, other types of dependencies can be highlighted. Two main cases are the dependency on model and the dependency on material. These cases are more practical than theoretical.

Indeed, two simulations can have no parameter in common, and still one can use an input from the other. This input can be the whole model for example: for two simulations dealing with the same structure, it is useless to do pre-processing (especially meshing) in both DVMs if the simulation mesh can be the same. Taking same approach, the application proposes an optional feature that allows specifying the type of mesh that is used for simulations (surface structural, volume structural, or environment). If two simulations use the same type of mesh, a dependency on model is proposed. Of course, this dependency is not obviously relevant (two simulations can use two surface structural meshes that are totally different), but the application suggests it to show that this dependency is a possibility.

Exceptions

	The same can happen for the material properties and for the post processing results: after a simulation, the shape of the model can be changed and the material properties can be modified by the engineer. If other DVMs need these parameters as inputs, a dependency is defined. All these dependencies can be modified manually. These exceptional in phase 2 define boundaries of application area of the method to build generic simulations dependencies.
Summary	Phase 2 "CAE Dependency Specification" develops a library of generic dependencies among simulations. The universal dependencies library helps to figure out most of the simulation dependencies irrespective of product, priority and development phase. Moreover, it identifies each and every dependency those are commonly ignored as it is difficult to identify them manually. In this phase, exceptional which are discussed are based on practices of automotive industry. It can differ for other manufacturing industries. All stated exceptions can be added and customized in dependency library as per industrial requirement. After identifying generic dependencies, it is transferred to next methods steps where a customized CAE network is developed using these dependencies.

Table 3. 3 Phase 2 CAE-Dependency Specification

3.3.3 CAE Network

Phase-3: CAE- Network

Introduction

A group of interconnected and non-interconnected simulation considering their dependencies and relation type among simulations for a particular system or product is known as CAE Network. Aftermath of phase 2 – "Dependency Specification", the generic relation is defined according to theoretical dependencies. The phase-3 CAE network is a customization of phase-2 for a particular industry or company. It includes products, development phases and simulation priorities.

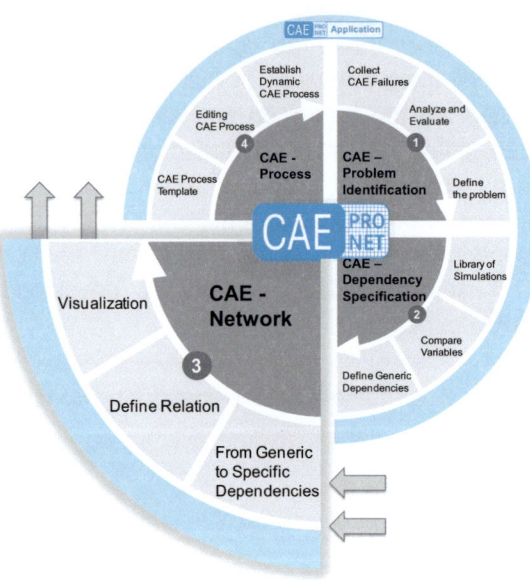

Figure 3. 12 Phase 3 of CAE-ProNet Methodology

	Phase 3 has further three steps. First is to transfer data from generic to specific. Then defining the relation considering requirement variable like product type. As a final point the sub-step "Visualization", this helps users to use the results of CAE Network in an appropriate way. Figure 3.12 demonstrates phase and steps to this method CAE-Network
Objective	The objective of Phase 3 is to adapt generic dependencies to build a CAE Network for that organization or work group. It makes existing data effectively and easily available to users, thus helps in reducing the complexity. Another benefit of this phase is to collaborate simulation teams. The outcome of CAE Network is reduction in load cases that are simplified and hardware testing based. Therefore, it improves the quality and reduces development cost. Furthermore, it visualizes dependencies in various forms to make it simple and comprehensive.
Steps	Prerequisites of Phase 3 are the list of products, development phases and priority with respect to simulations and load cases. A simplified procedure is given below to create CAE Network **Step-1 From Generic to Specific Dependencies:** • Import a list of products with its digital validation requirement. • Repeat the process to import digital validation requirement with respect to development phase and priorities according to load cases. These are prerequisites to build industry specific CAE Network.

| **Steps** | • Select a product filter the simulation and its load cases according to the selected product. This process is called filtering. (the filtering algorithm is elaborated in next Phase "CAE Process" 3.3.4)

• Repeat the filtering process for development phase and as well as for priority.

• Finally, a list of simulations and its load case for specific product, development phase and priority are prepared

Step-2 Define Relation:

Factors to define a relation between simulations and its load cases are demonstrated in figure 3.13.

• To define a relation for that particular product, first select a load case. Define its dependent load case according to the generic dependencies. Repeat the process as there is possibility to have more than one dependency. ,

• According to the dependency, define the mapping methods. The generic dependencies state that the mapping is required or not. The type of mapping i.e. various interpolation methods have to be selected and defined in this phase according to quality requirement.

• Define the workflow between load cases. The workflow possibilities are parallel or sequential. Parallel is used when there is a co-simulation or data are exchange in one time. Sequential is used wherever one simulation needs results or output of other simulation. |

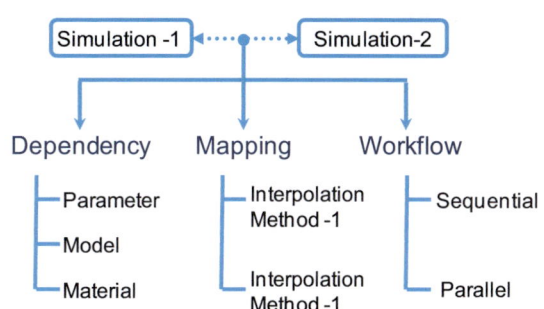

Figure 3. 13 Factors to define relation among simulations

Other parameters to define a relation between simulations are approximate modeling and optimization time of the load case for that particular product in chosen development phase.

Step 3 – Visualization:

There are various ways of visualization. The way in this method is used is the matrix format. It has advantage of simplicity, ease of use, quicker and all in one view. [SaDa-05]

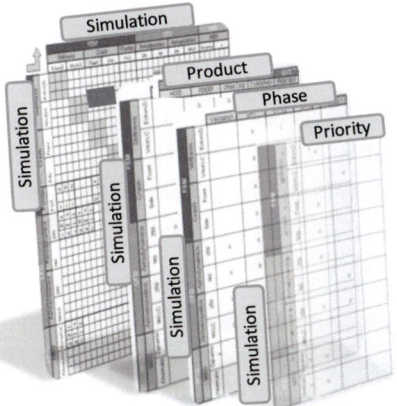

Figure 3. 14 Relation Matrices

Steps	Figure 3.14 shows the various dependencies between simulation – simulation, simulations – product, simulation – development phases and simulation-priorities. Visualize the results of data mining of relations among simulations, products, development phases and priorities.
Examples	Considering the same example of aerodynamics and stiffness to explain the steps of CAE Network. The figure 3.15 shows the aerodynamic effect of vehicle side.  Figure 3. 15 Aerodynamics effect on vehicle"s door side. [ATZ-07] As seen in last phase "Dependency Specification", the generic relation between aerodynamics and stiffness simulation. In this session "CAE Network", thse focus is onto specific product as well as on specific load case on aerodynamics and stiffness analysis. Product, development phase and priority list with respect to their simulations or load case list is required as a prerequisite to develop CAE Network. Selecting Motorhood as a product, development phase-2 and priority level 2 as load case priority. After filtering process, specific load cases for these conditions are deliberated for further steps

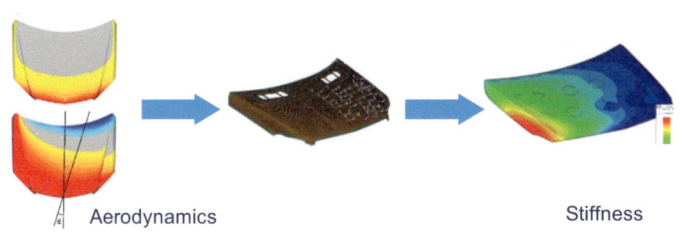

Aerodynamics   Stiffness

Figure 3. 16 Motorhood Simulations

Left figure 3.16 – Pressure on Motorhood due to Side Wind calculated by Aerodynamic Simulation and Right Picture-Stiffness Analysis result due to wind pressure on Motorhood.

Add a new load case in stiffness analysis for Motorhood. From the generic dependency list, it shows Aerodynamics and its load cases as counter-dependent. Choosing a load case of side wind–250 km/hr it shows that the dependency types are parameter (pressure distribution) and Model (FE-Pre-process Model), as shown in Figure 3.17

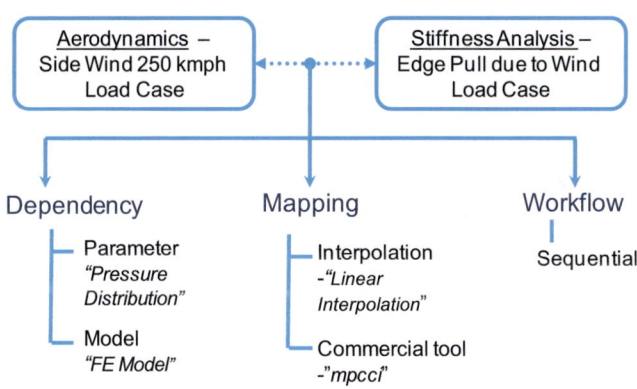

Figure 3. 17 Relation defined for Aerodynamics and Stiffness Analysis

Linear Interpolation is used for mapping and sequential workflow from aerodynamics to stiffness. Other variables of time are company specific as it dependents on various hardware and software used in the company.

The CAE ProNet methodology ideally works on single product simulation dependencies. Dependencies among Products w.r.t simulations have to customize manually from Generic dependencies. Product to Product relations are specific. Thus, this feature can be done manually in this methodology. An example of product – product relation w.r.t simulation is given in figure 3.18. Two products – Air conditioner and Car Front Glass have close relation for defrosting simulation. Velocity Streamline plot from air condition that heat flow of an air conditioner is required for defrosting simulation for car glass. Such kind of dependencies have to manually defined or customized in CAE-ProNet methodology.

Exception

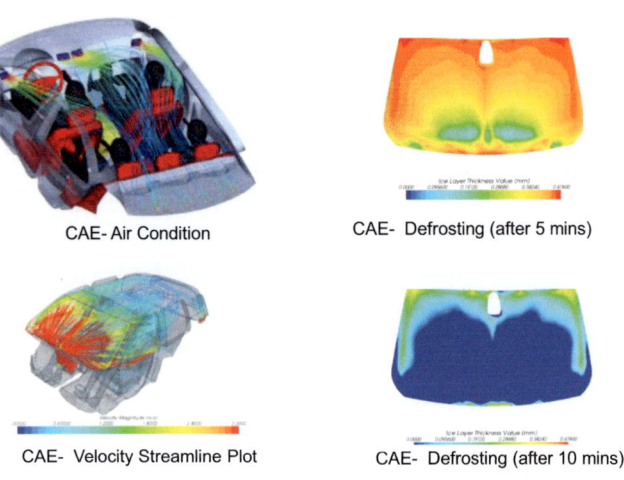

CAE- Air Condition   CAE- Defrosting (after 5 mins)

CAE- Velocity Streamline Plot   CAE- Defrosting (after 10 mins)

Figure 3. 18 Defrost Simulation on Windshield

Summary	Phase 3 "CAE Network" is a major part of CAE ProNet methodology and truly constructive for industrial use. Customization of generic dependencies, filtering generic data with respect to product, phase and load case priority gives a concrete solution that helps simulations engineers to build and use CAE Network. CAE Network results in reduced number of simplified and hardware dependent simulations. Moreover, it improves accessibility of existing digital data that leads to simulation quality improvement.

Table 3. 4 Phase 3 CAE-Network

3.3.4 CAE Process

Phase-4: CAE- Process	
Introduction	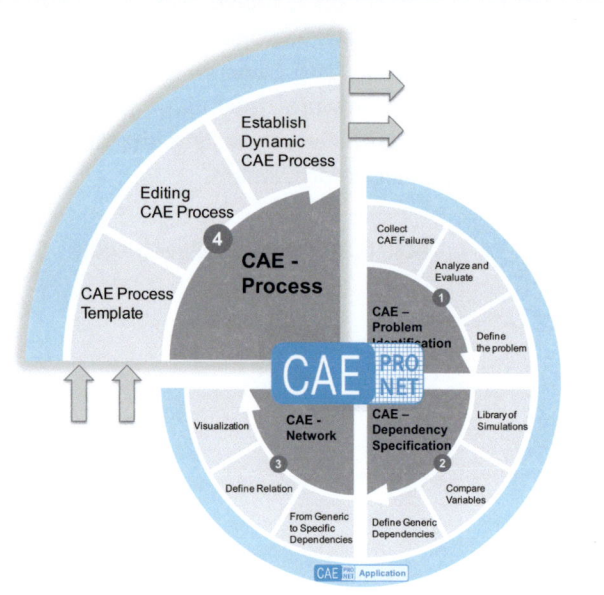Figure 3. 19 Phase 4 of CAE-ProNet Methodology
Objective	Major objective of CAE process is to describe optimized dynamic CAE operations considering dependencies among simulations. CAE process is described with higher granularity. The first level is among simulations (E.g. aerodynamics to stiffness), second level is between simulations load cases (Aerodynamics/Wind Load Case to Stiffness/Edge Pull Load Case). Finally, a third or bottom level is the process in which load cases from pre-processing to post processing are elaborated. It contains types of files, results, graphs, pictures etc. saved in simulation database. The three levels of CAE Process are shown in Figure 3.20

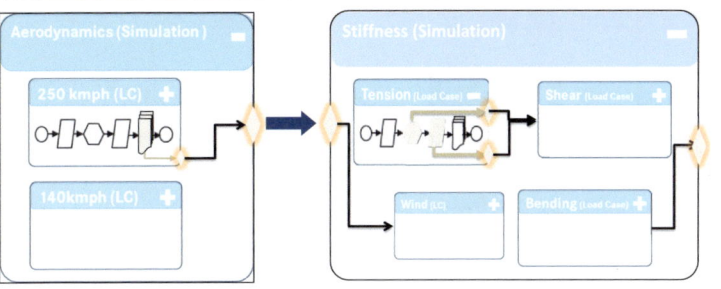

Figure 3. 20 Levels of CAE Process

Objective

Algorithm

The phase-4 receives dependencies matrices (Design Structure Matrices) as inputs. An algorithm which is used to describe a process is given below :).

The algorithm to describe process using dependency matrix:

According to graph theory, the interdependency relationships among simulations that are defined in phase-3 CAE-network can be plotted to a various matrices (section 3.3.3). The matrix is called Design Structure Matrix (DSM), in which rows and columns are corresponding to simulations. The DSM (Fig. 3.21) associated with a directed graph is a binary square matrix with m rows and columns, and n non-zero elements, where m is the number of nodes and n is the number of directed lines connecting these nodes in the directed graph. If there exists a direct line from node j to node I, then the value of element aij (column j, row i) is unity (or marked with an X). Otherwise, it would be the value of the element.

Definition-1 matrix to process: given are a set A with n elements and a set B with m elements. Then the dependency structure matrix DnXm between A and B can be defined as:

Algorithm

$Dij=$ {0, $ai \perp\!\!\!\perp aj$

{1, $if\ ai{\rightarrow}aj$

Here "ai $\perp\!\!\!\perp$ aj" denotes that element bj is independent on ai while "ai $\rightarrow$ aj" denotes that aj is dependent on ai (aj needs information from ai as the input information). D is so-called Dependency structure matrix. Fig. 3.21 and 3.22 shows a classic DSM and type of activity relationships. [HsTL-08] [ChHu-07].

$D =$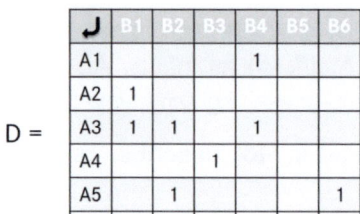

Figure 3. 22 A Classic DSM

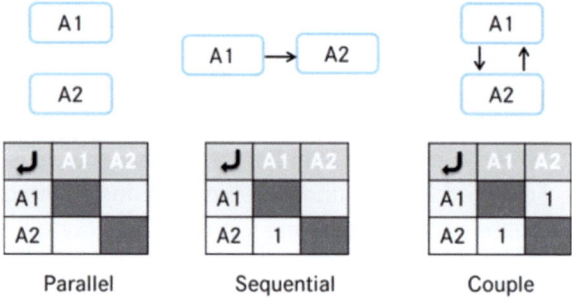

Figure 3. 21 Three Types of activity relationships

Algorithm

According to above definition, a directed process or graph describing the relationships between simulations can be mapped to a DSM further. Through analyzing and planning method of DSM, one can obtain an optimized CAE process showing direct graph to CAE process.[Brow-08]

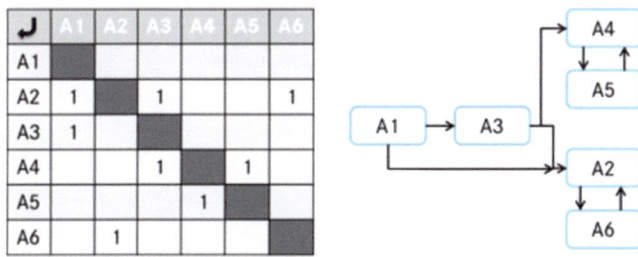

Figure 3. 23 DSM to Process

Definition -2 Filter Matrix: Filtering is done using scalar multiplication of matrices A = (aij) and a scalar r gives a product r A of the same size as A. The entries of r A are given by

$$(r\mathbf{A})_{ij} = r \cdot a_{ij}.$$

Selecting "r" as B1 for case 1 and B2 for case 2 from Martix D.

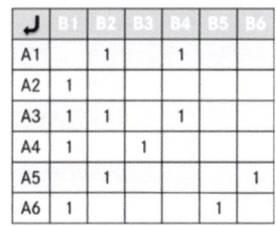

↲	A1	A2	A3	A4	A5	A6
A1						
A2	1		1			1
A3	1					
A4			1		1	
A5				1		
A6		1				

Matrix [A]

∩

↲	B1	B2	B3	B4	B5	B6
A1		1		1		
A2	1					
A3	1	1		1		
A4	1		1			
A5		1				1
A6	1				1	

Matrix [D]

Algorithm	For case 1: Matrix A filtered and results are : 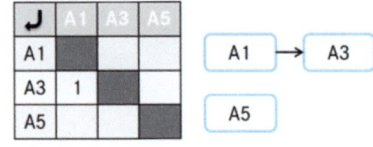 For case 2: Matrix A filtered and results are : B1.[A]= [A²]
Steps	**Step-1 CAE Process Template:** • Using the above algorithm to describe a process via design structure matrix, CAE process template is developed. • The CAE process template consists of processes among simulation, load cases and computation file dependencies. **Step-2 Editing CAE Process:** • The CAE process template can be edited according to the dynamics requirements. • Filtering the matrix using Definition 2 mentioned above. Process can be edited w.r.t product, development phase or /and priority.

Steps	**Step-3 Establish Dynamic CAE Process:** • After altering the CAE process according to the requirement, CAE process is established. • Simulation engineers follow the process and take inputs data according to process. After successfully accomplishing the simulation task they save the data in database. • Quality of simulation results are rated using color-coding. Outcome of CAE process enable system to generate quality reports that are used for problem identification in loop-2 of CAE ProNet methodology. n illustration of CAE process is shown in figure 3.24. The picture represents various simulation and load cases. Types of dependency is shown with 3 different colors
Summary	Phase 4 "CAE Process" plays major role in continuous development and implementation of CAE ProNet methodology and truly constructive for competitive industrial application. Automatic generation of CAE Process template helps user to build and edit according to the requirement. The output of CAE Process varies person to person. Dynamic process indicates the current process which helps in controlling and optimizing the process at right time. Managers are benefited to have an overview of process and simultaneously keeping an eye of process quality. On the other hand simulation engineers are benefited by receiving right data at right time. Moreover information on quality of data received helps simulation engineers to understand the process.

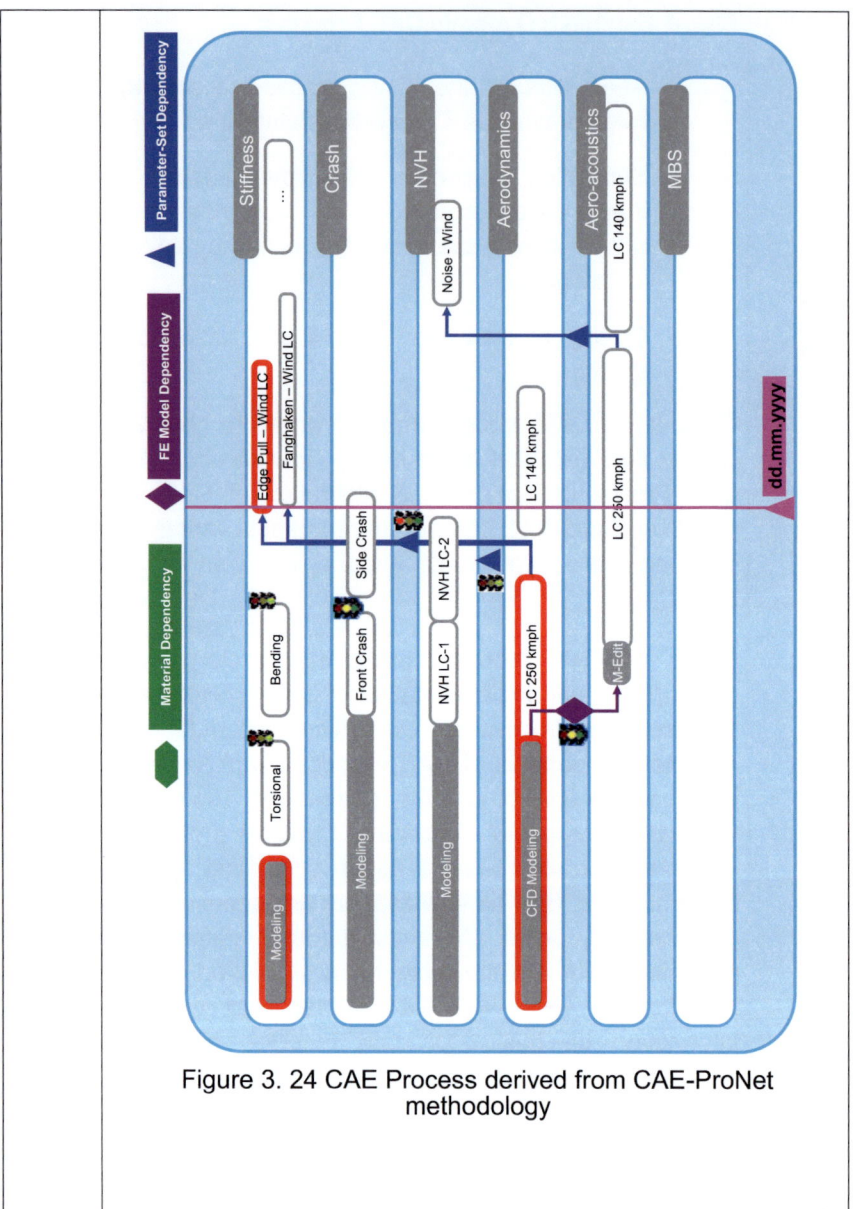

Figure 3. 24 CAE Process derived from CAE-ProNet methodology

Table 3. 5 Phase 4 - CAE-Process

3.4 CAE-ProNet Application

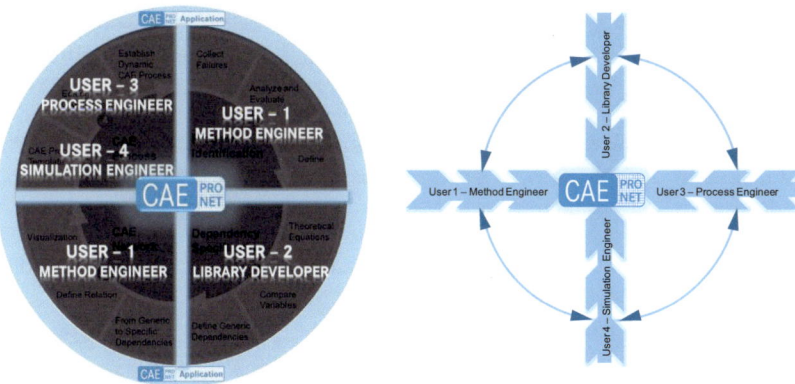

Figure 3. 25 CAE-ProNet Application Users (right) and their active phases (left)

In previous section 3.3 "Methodology Description" each phase of CAE-ProNet methodology is described. CAE-ProNet Application with encircle the CAE-ProNet methodology is illustrated in this section. The application aids to define Users role and actions.

There are four major user types in the CAE-ProNet methodology. User - 1 "Method Engineer" is active in method-step 1 "CAE Problem Identification" and in method-step 3 "CAE – Network", User -2 "Library Developer" is active in method-step 2 "CAE Dependency Specification" and finally in method-step 4 CAE Process User 3 "Process Engineer" and User-4 "Simulation Engineers" plays a major part.

Definition Method Engineer: Method engineering is the discipline to construct new methods from existing know-how. It focuses on "the design, construction and evaluation of methods, techniques and support tools for development". Furthermore method engineering "wants to improve the usefulness of systems development methods by creating an adaptation framework whereby methods are created to match specific situations". The methods engineer can be one of the simulation engineers that define the simulation and load case execution method.

Definition Library Developer: An engineer or mathematician who is responsible for developing simulation library and extracting theoretical dependencies by comparing common parameters.

Definition Process Engineer: An engineer focuses on the operation, control, and optimization of organization processes through the aid of systematic computer-based methods.

Definition Simulation Engineer: Simulation engineers are responsible for the study concerned with constructing mathematical models and quantitative analysis techniques and using computers to analyze and solve scientific problems. In practical use, they use application of computer simulation and other forms of simulation or computation to problems in various scientific disciplines.

Roles and actions of each user are defined in this session. Figure 3.26 is a general format to explain motive, resources and actions of each user type. ◇ A Diamond icon is used for motivation, ▭ a multi document icon is used for resources and ▷ a chevron icon represents actions of user.

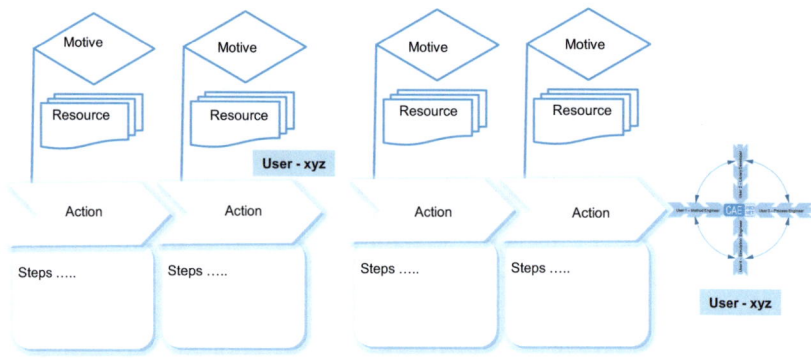

Figure 3. 26 General structure of User Actions

3.4.1 User 1 – "Method Engineer"

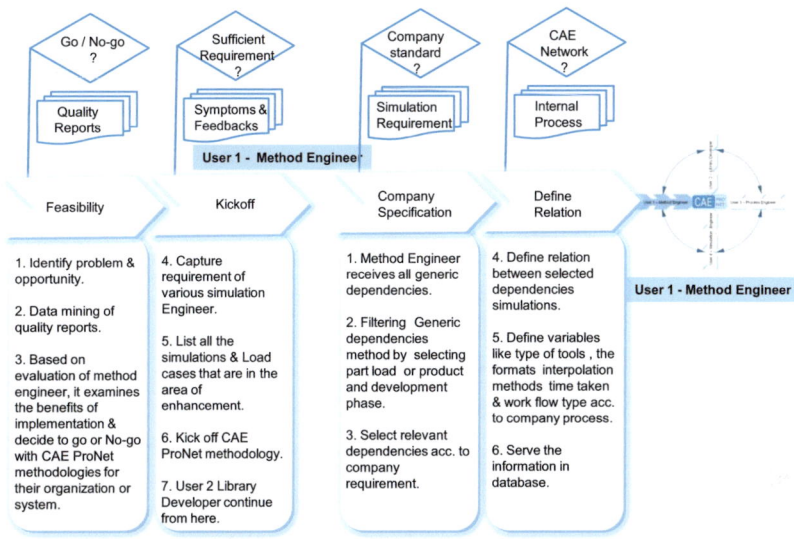

Figure 3. 27 User 1 - Method Engineer Actions

Major actions of method engineers are given below and detailed steps are illustrated in Figure 3.27.

Feasibility: Aim of this action is to decide whether the CAE-ProNet methodology is feasible for that system or not. Method engineer is responsible for elaborating and examining the expected benefits of CAE-ProNet in their system. Detailed steps are given in figure 3.27.

Kickoff: After feasibility decision, the methodology kickoff with collecting requirements and addressing the area of implementation. Both actions feasibility and kickoff are in the phase of method-step 1 "CAE Problem identification". Feasibility and kickoff actions are for phase 1. The method engineer is active phase 1 and phase 3 as shown in figure 3.25.

Company Specification: In Phase 3 – CAE-Network, Method engineer receives generic dependencies and method engineer is responsible for customizing generic dependencies according to company specification.

Define Relation: A definition relation between simulation using internal requirement and standards is the final action of method engineer.

3.4.2 User 2 – "Library Developer"

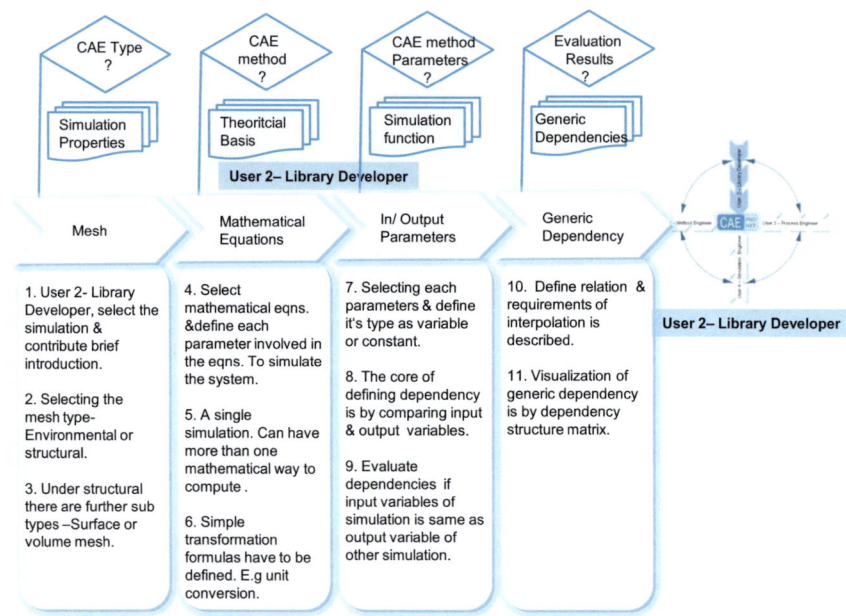

Figure 3. 28 User 2 - Library Develop Actions

Major actions of library developer are given below and detailed steps are illustrated in Figure 3.28.

Mesh: Simulations are categorized according to the type which is defined by mesh type. Library Developer collects and categorizes simulation and load cases. Detailed steps are given in figure 3.28.

Mathematical Equations: Core of library developing is by collecting the simulation analytical way i.e. the mathematical formulation of simulation. As in section 3.3.2, there can be many analytical ways to perform individual simulation. Focus of this section is to collect parameters from equations. General parameters of all equations of that particular simulation are same.

In/Output Parameters: Mathematical formulations are compared with the various types of parameters like input, output, constant etc. to define generic dependencies.

Generic Dependency: Generic dependencies are automatically evaluated and can be visualized as structure design matrix. All these above actions are accomplished in method-step 2 "CAE Dependency Specification".

3.4.3 User 3 – Process Engineer

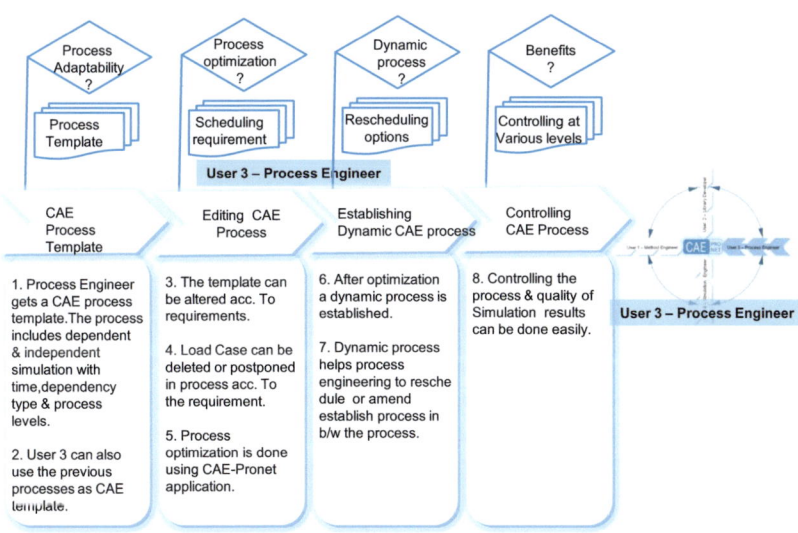

Figure 3. 29 User 3 - Process Engineer Actions

Major actions of method engineer are given below and detailed steps are illustrated in Figure 3.29

CAE Process Template: Process engineer receives a process template generated by an algorithm described in section 3.3.4. Process template includes dependent, independent simulation, processing time, dependency type and levels. CAE process template includes all existing dependencies irrespective of product priority etc.

Editing CAE Process: According to the company requirements and priorities, process engineer can alter CAE process. Exceptional cases can be edited in this step and balance analytical and practical solutions.

Dynamic CAE Process: After altering, a dynamic process is established that updated automatically at every quality gate of development process. Dynamic states that it gives update at every step. Quality of simulation and process stages are highlighted.

Controlling CAE Process: Process engineer can easily controls the process. Using dynamic process, the editing can be possible in between the development phase. All above actions of process engineer are performed in method-step 4 "CAE –Process".

3.4.4 User 4 – Simulation Engineer

Major actions of simulation engineer are given below and detailed steps are illustrated in Figure 3.30.

Notification: A notification is received to simulation engineer containing process start and how to execute simulation according to the standards. Simulation engineer can plan his/her task accordingly. Notification includes quality of data received from dependent simulation. Users can add comments after sending accomplished tasks.

For Pre-Processing: To start with reprocessing, simulation engineer needs data to compute, dependent data can be directly received by CAE ProNet methodology that helps to work effectively.

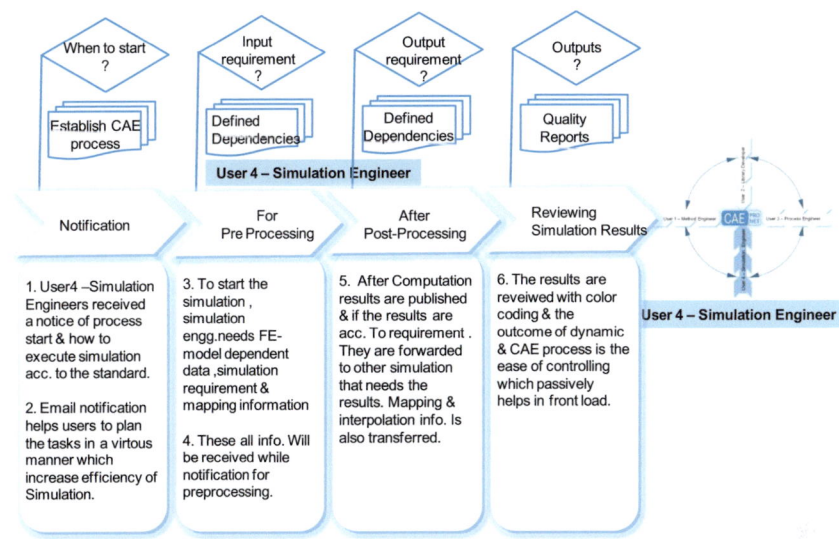

Figure 3. 30 User 4 - Simulation Engineer Actions

After post processing: After computing and post processing, the relevant and dependent data can be directly exported as notified in action 1.

Reviewing Simulation results: Major task of simulation engineer is to review the quality of results using color-coding. All above actions of process engineer are performed in method-step 4 "CAE –Process". These actions help to get data faster with enhanced quality. Thereby, it contributes in project front loading.

The methodology is in continuous closed loop. In next loop, user does not have to perform all above steps. It depends on optimization involved in that loop. Same Process can also be used for various projects. All above actions are accumulated and Implemented in an application described in chapter 4. Use case diagram, sequential diagram and activity diagram are given in Annex B.

3.5 Results of CAE-ProNet

3.5.1 Scientific Added Value

The scientific added values of CAE-ProNet methodology are as follows:

- This method to identify generic dependencies among simulations is unique and vastly required. State of art industrial as well as scientific clearly illustrated a need of method to identify dependencies among simulations (as shown in Table 2.8). Identifying dependencies using theoretical approach open paths to link vast field of simulations including mechanical, electric, mechatronic etc. User can add simulations as much as he needs for build CAE-Network for his workgroup or organization as elaborated in phase 2 "CAE- Dependency Specification".

- The results of generic dependencies can be applied in various workgroups and organization. Library of simulation is a onetime effort and can be used for various workgroups. Dependencies highlighted are suggested as per the CAE-ProNet and user can edit or delete or add manually new dependencies within the CAE-ProNet methodology.

- An innovative way to manage and share existing knowledge, experience and data in vehicle life cycle. Dynamic CAE Process is a step ahead to standard processes where tracking and controlling is very difficult especially in CAE. Apart from deadline controlling in CAE Process, quality of simulation data flow is a key factor. This innovative way to highlight CAE Process including high granularity helps workgroups to manage and control CAE data workflow.

- An efficient validation phase of vehicle life cycle management to learn from previous errors and continuous improves quality of simulations. CAE-ProNet methodology is a continuous process in Life cycle management. Lesson learnt at each loop facilitate in improvement of CAE system.

- Efficient building of dependencies helps to pinpoint redundancy in whole CAE operations performed.

- Reduction in CAE System complexity. Challenges of simulation data management (SDM) are not same as of product/electric data management. The methodology supports SDM in CAE complexity reduction.

3.5.2 Industrial Added Value

CAE-ProNet methodology is developed focusing to improve digital validation of products. Added values of CAE-ProNet are as follows:

- Benefits of reducing time of searching and collecting useful existing data are realized by simulation engineers. CAE-ProNet networks existing data and improves system transparency which leads to enhance effectiveness of simulation engineers.

- A vital benefit for automotive manufacturer is by improving the quality of simulations by receiving actual and detailed simulation data. The results carried out by this computational are of better approximation and closer to real results.

- Identified and analyzed the failures due to dependent simplified load cases in vehicle validation phase avoid future failures.

- CAE-ProNet network assists dependent simulation to use the digital results of its dependent simulation. Thereby, it reduced the dependency on Hardware prototypes which is used to evaluate simplified load cases. Reducing dependency affects in dipping development cost.

- Creating a common understanding and knowledge basis of interpolation and mapping tools reduces redundant mapping tools.

- CAE-Process with higher granularity benefits managers for process understanding and controlling.

- System responsible get an overview about all relevant validations, dependencies, mapping and process related to the considered system. Thus, it benefits manufacturer by managing complexity of vast simulations.

- Immense potentials are realized by functionalities of CAE-ProNet's digital to collaborated teams and various users groups.

These benefits meet the objectives and expected benefits which are described in Chapter-1 and generates sustainable success for automotive organizations. All objectives and benefits are also verified using an automotive practical example to authenticate the applicability and sustainability of CAE-ProNet in a complex automotive environment.

3.6 Chapter Summary

This chapter introduces a new methodology called CAE-ProNet which is based on evaluation results of existing industrial as well as scientific methodologies. Phase 2 – "CAE Dependency Specification" helps to build a library of simulations and extracting generic dependencies among simulation. Generic dependencies are aimed to be implemented in various organizations. This method is unique and highly required to build holistic digital system. Afterwards, CAE-ProNet methodology delivers possibilities to apply business requirement and customization in constructing CAE-Network from generic dependencies. Phase 4 of CAE-ProNet methodology illustrated an optimized process that can be established and implemented in an organization. Furthermore, it opens door by defining stipulated roles with actions and goals to achieve. The chapter concludes itself by providing benefits in terms of scientific and industrial aspects.

4 IMPLEMENTATION OF CAE-ProNet

4.1 Introduction

Last chapter was dedicated to explain steps and procedures for CAE ProNet methodology to solve the challenges stated in chapter-1. The drive of this chapter is implementation of methods to realize the methodology described in chapter 3.

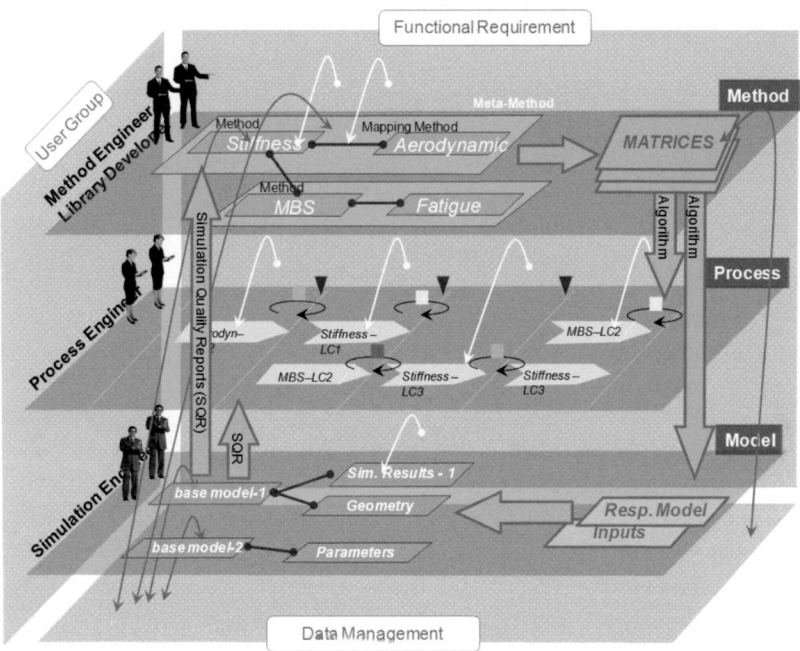

Figure 4. 1 People and Organization structure of CAE ProNet

CAE ProNet application approach is divided in three levels and four user groups. The three layers are method, process and model. The user groups responsible for method layer are library and methods engineer. Process engineer is represents in process layer and finally simulation engineer take care of model layer. The figure 4.1 represents the practical approach of CAE-ProNet in an organization.

A digital solution of CAE-ProNet has been implemented using methods and procedures described in chapter-3. The application is known as CAE-ProNet application has been developed using Visual Basics for frontend and MySQL for backend. Requirements, objectives, solution, benefits and further steps of the applications are described in this chapter.

4.2 Implementation of CAE-ProNet Application

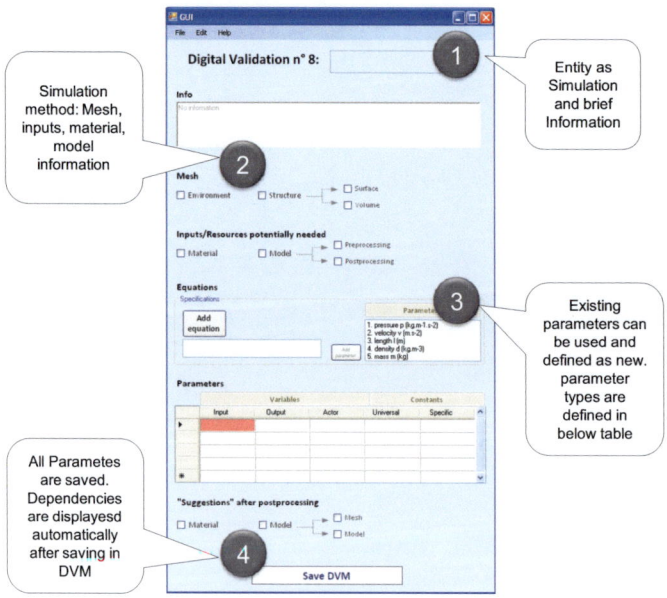

Figure 4. 2 Library Developer - GUI

4.2.1 User Interface for Library Developer

Library of simulations and dependencies is a root of CAE-ProNet, as it helps to build the CAE Network which leads to CAE process. The focus is to build and use a generic method which can be executed in other organization or workgroups.

Figure 4.2 is screen capture of developed software application prototype which allows creating library of simulations and dependencies. The logic used for developing this method is explained in section 3.3.1. This application gather parameter as mentioned in method as saves in data bank. This application is able to generate a report in the way of matrix describing simulations and their interdependencies. Table 4.1 and 4.2 depicts the implementation of existing simulations.

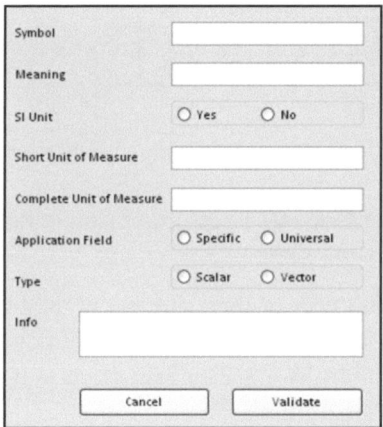

Figure 4. 3 Library Developer GUI for Units

Figure 4.3 is the interface containing the fields to fill the parameter information that allows the creation of an element of the library of parameters. An element is distinguished from the others thanks to its symbol and meaning that are unique. The field "SI Unit" aims at knowing if the parameter is one of SI Units. The other types of parameters have a short unit that is in common practice in engineering. The fields "Application Field", "Type" and "Info" are optional information and not needed for the creation of simulation. The application field specifies if the parameter is specific to a simulation, or a universal constant.

/	Sim-2		...		Aero-dynamics		Stiffness		...		Sim-n	
Sim-1	/		W	T	W	T	W	T	W	T	W	T
			M	P	M	P	M	P	M	P	M	P
...	W	T	/		W	T	W	T	W	T	W	T
	M	P			M	P	M	P	M	P	M	P
Aero-dynamics	W	T	W	T	/		Workflow / Type		W	T	W	T
	M	P	M	P			Mapping / Parameter		M	P	M	P
NVH	W	T	W	T	W	T	/		W	T	W	T
	M	P	M	P	M	P			M	P	M	P
...	W	T	W	T	W	T	W	T	/		W	T
	M	P	M	P	M	P	M	P				
Sim-n	W	T	W	T	W	T	W	T			/	
	M	P	M	P	M	P	M	P	Aero-dynamics			

	Stiffness	
Aerodynamics -> Stiffness	Parameter	
	Yes	Pressure

Example of dependency visualization

Table 4. 1 General Structure of Dependency Matrix

Workflow: Specify the flow of data. An arrow rightwards signifies that the data is transferred from the DVM in the left column to the DVM in the top row. A double-arrow signifies that there is a strong coupling: a co-simulation can be performed.

Type: Specify the type of dependency: material, model, and/or parameter. If there is no dependency on parameter, the lower box is not filled.

Mapping: Specify if a mapping is needed from one DVM to the other, especially when the mesh of one DVM is different from the mesh of the other DVM (for instance, from CFD to FEA).

Parameter: If there is a dependency on parameter, specify the common parameter(s) between both DVMs.

	Aeroacoustics	Aerodynamics	Stiffness	Fatigue	NVH	Multibody	Forming	Crash	Thermal	Electrical
Electrical					Pa, In+U / Seq, No			Pa, Te / Seq, No		—
Thermal	Pa+, Mo, Te / Par, No	Pa+, Mo, Te / Par, No							—	
Crash				Pa, Fo+Ve / Seq, No			Pa+Mo+, Ma, σ. / Seq, No	—		
Forming							—	Pa, Te / Seq, Yes		
Multibody					Mo, x / S, No	—				
NVH	Pa, Pr / Seq, Yes	Pa, Pr / Seq, Yes	Mod, x / Par, No	Mo, x / Par, No	—	Pa, X(t) / Seq, No	Mo, x / Seq, No			
Fatigue	Pa, Pr / Seq, Yes	Pa, Pr / Seq, Yes	Mo+Ma, x / Par, No	—	Mo, x / Par, No	Pa, Pr+Fo / Seq, No		Pa+Mo+, Ma, σ. / Seq, No	Pa, Te / Seq, Yes	
Stiffness	Pa, Pr / Seq, Yes	Pa, Pr / Seq, Yes	—	Mo+Ma, x / Par, No	Mo, x / Par, No	Pa, Pr+Fo / Seq, No		Pa+Mo+, Ma, σ. / Seq, No	Pa, Tem / Seq, Yes	
Aerodynamics	M, x / Seq, No	—							Pa+, Mo, Te / Par, No	
Aeroacoustics	—								Pa+, Mo, Te / Par, No	

Table 4. 2 Implemented - Dependency Matrix

Abbreviations used in above table:

Seq : Sequential, Par : Parallel, Pa : Parameter, Mo : Model, Ma: Material, Pr : Pressure. Te :   Temperature, Fo : Force, In : Intensity, U : Tension, σ : Tensile Strength and X(t) : Position

Benefits of GUI – Library Developer:

- Implemented dependency matrix can be used in various organizations and workgroups.

- Highlights each and every single dependency that is mostly neglected due to minor effect of dependents.

- Facilitates the choice of mapping tool later which helps in building standard mapping and interpolation methods.

- Single time investment. After first implementation, workgroups can reuse the results.

Statement 4.1: This section achieves objective 3.1.2 "Extracting Dependencies" mentioned in section 3.1. The current method, evaluate dependencies among simulations on theoretical bases. The library model is generic and could be implemented in any organization that applies simulations to validate design of product.

4.2.2 User Interface for Method Engineer

Figure 4.4 is a screen capture of Graphical User Interface of Method Engineer. Bubble-1 represents the frame of Simulation-Tree. Simulation tree is divided into three various kind of simulation: Structural Validation, Fluid Validation and Miscellaneous Validation. Bubble-2 represents lists of products, development phase and Load case priorities. Bubble-3 represents the tabs of parameter used to define the relation between load cases. For example parameter like Loadcase name, dependency type, mapping and time. After saving all parameter to data base, the next steps can be followed to visualization and process as shown by Bubble-4.

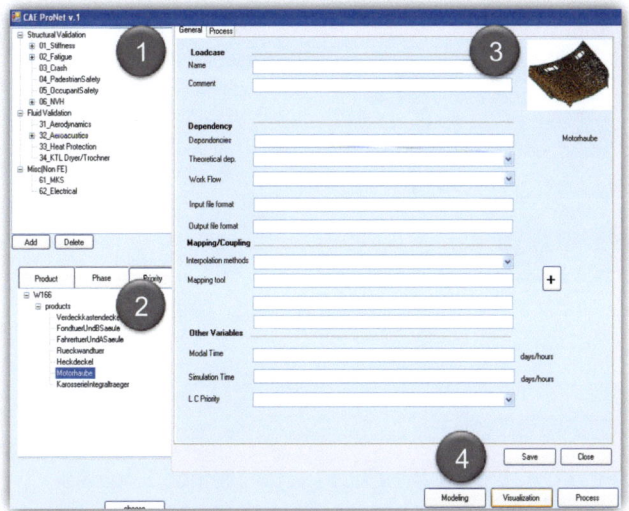

Figure 4. 4 User Interface -1 for Method Engineer

In figure 4.5 Bubble-1 and 2 have the same functionalities as in figure 4.4. Bubble -3 shows the various forms of matrices which represents dependencies among LCs-LCs, LCs-Product, LC-Development Phase and LCs-Priority.

Major functionalities and benefits of Method Engineer using the given GUI are elaborated below.

- Importing simulation dependencies from library of simulation and dependencies.

- Filter Load cases (LCs) with respect to specific and existing products, development phase and LC priority.

- Define new dependencies using imported theoretical dependencies.

- Add, remove and/or modify load cases (LCs).

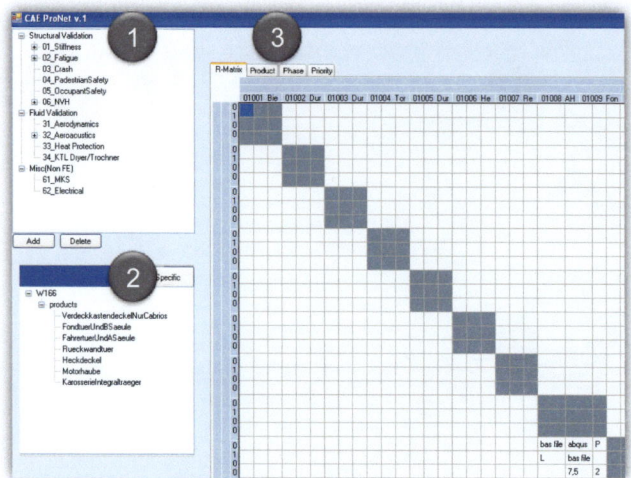

Figure 4. 5 User Interface - 2 for Method Engineer

- Define relation between LCs to LCs according to organization requirements and standards.

- Save all information into persistent memory.

- Visualization of various dependencies using matrix format.

Benefits of Method Researcher functionalities:

- **Adaptability** – From generic dependencies to particular organization or workgroup specific LC dependencies can be described and visualized.

- **Systemization** – CAE Network can be developed and reuse for upcoming models.

- **Managing Complexity** – Managing complex structure of simulation and simulation interdependent information.

- **Transparency** – dependencies between simulations and load cases can be viewed by each user. It helps users to understand the complete process.

- **Flexibility** – simulation and load cases can be updated easily.

Statement 4.2: This section attains the objective 3.1.3 "Team Collaboration" mentioned in section 3.1. The above method elaborates the customization of generic dependencies for particular workgroups. It enables to collaborate various simulation departments, teams and engineers.

4.2.3 User Interface for Process Engineer

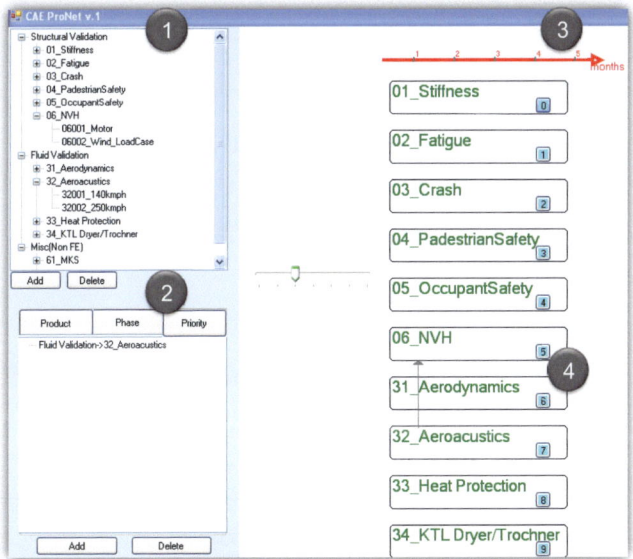

Figure 4. 6 User Interface for Process Engineer

Above figure 4.6 is a screen capture of GUI of Process Engineer. Bubble-1 and 2 shows the same functionalities as in figure 4.3. Bubble-3 represents the frame of time line and Bubble-4 shows the frame of CAE Process with simulation and its load cases. Major functionalities and benefits of Method Researcher using the given GUI are elaborated below.

Summary of Process Engineer functionalities:

- Generate automatically CAE process template according to dependencies.

- CAE process template can be altered acc. To the current requirements to establish a standard CAE Process.

- Three levels of CAE process can be described a)Simulation levels (NVH – Aeroacoustics) b) LCs level (NVH / Wind LC – Aeroacoustics/140 kmph LC) and c)Inside LCs (Pre-processing, solving, Post-Processing, Evaluation…)

- Reuse of CAE template is also possible.

- Established CAE Process can be updated according to the time line and data saved.

- CAE Process gives information on mapping process and quality reports of simulations.

Benefits of Process Engineer functionalities:

- **Better Controlling** – Shorter and elaborated Quality gates including quality reports helps to control better for process manager.

- **Transparency** – User gets information on quality reports and complete CAE process which aids to know the quality of complete process.

- **Traceability** – Errors can be easily traced as dependencies and quality of simulations is transparent which helps to point out error prone areas.

Statement 4.3: This section achieves the objective 3.1.4 "Optimizing existing process" mentioned in section 3.1. The above illustrated method describes and establishes an optimized CAE process including interdependencies among simulation and their load cases.

4.2.4 User Interface for Simulation Engineer

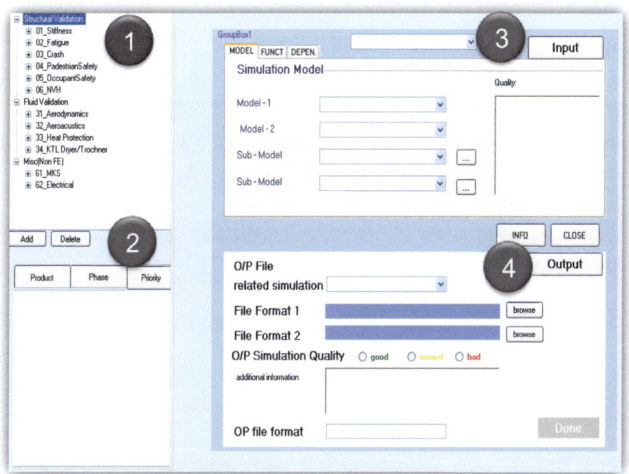

Figure 4. 7 User Interface for Simulation Engineer

Above figure 4.7 is a screen capture of GUI for Simulation Engineer. Bubble-1 and 2 shows the same functionalities as in figure 4.6. Bubble-3 represents the frame of input. After login simulations engineer gets information on input data he/she needs from other simulation. Dependent file and information like FE-model, material or parameters from other simulations can be imported directly from this frame. If data imported data is not available, dependency is not highlighted. And if data is available it highlights data and quality of simulation data received.

Bubble-4 demonstrates the frame of output. After performing computation, simulation engineer can save files that are required for another simulations in particular format. It suggest engineer to save in that particular format so that mapping can be performed automatically in batch mode or receiver can do mapping with that format. This information is well explained and elaborated in CAE Process. The GUI Simulation engineer helps simulation engineers to perform more efficient by receiving and delivering the files quicker and smoother. Major functionalities and benefits of Simulation Engineer using the given GUI are elaborated below.

Summary Simulation Engineer functionalities:

- Simulation engineers can access easily the relevant data. Managing data access supports to decrease the time on searching relevant data.

- Simulation engineer gets automatically inputs as dependent data.

- The quality of simulation results can be rated with comments.

- Simulation results are saved in Simulation data management through this application.

- Possibility to do interpolation automatically by batch mode using this application.

Benefits of Simulation Engineer functionalities:

- **Save time** – Simulation engineers don't have to search or arrange their input files.

- **Better Managing** – The quality of CAE process can be controlled by process engineers.

- **Reduce workload** – mapping can be done automatically.

Statement 4.4: This section explains the attainment of major objectives of reducing complexity and save time. The above method elaborates to work seamless on established CAE Process. It also supports to identify problems by collecting and evaluating quality reports generated by simulation engineers.

4.2.5 Interface of CAE-ProNet Application to Simulation Data Management

The explicit tasks and role of Simulation data management (SDM) within the Life Cycle management or xDM is not clearly defined. The functionality of CAE is not only product or system design verification, but simultaneously dimensioning and determination of design constraints. SDM become a data source for other domains in addition to managing the gathered information; including geometry, material, connectivity, and so on. Therefore, SDM system not only has to manage different types of data, but also with significantly different structures (functional vs. manufacturing) and has to provide mappings between them. [Baue-10]

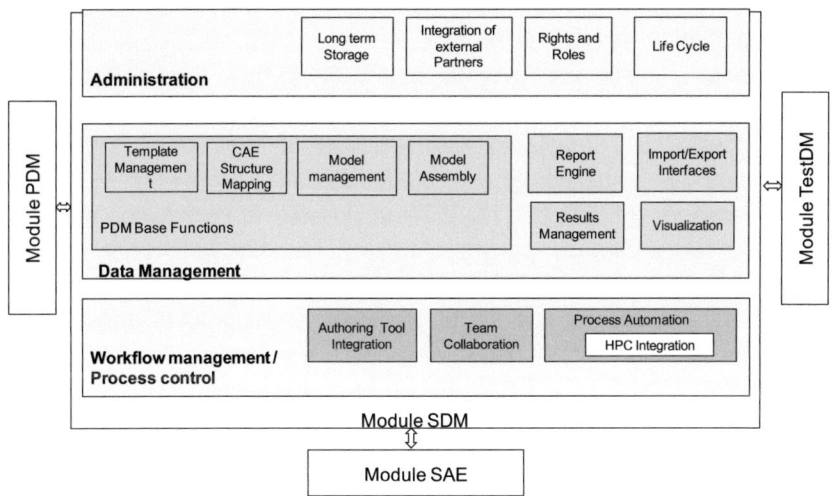

Figure 4. 8 Core Functionalities of SDM [SDM-10]

Figure 4.8 is the "Big Picture" of SDM with core functionalities. The SDM functionalities are divided in three major fields: Administration, Data management and workflow management and Process Control. CAE-ProNet lies in workflow management and process control. The core functionalities belong to workflow management's "Team Collaboration" module. Some features of CAE-ProNet also cover Data management's modules like Results management, visualization and Import/Export Interfaces.

Interfacing CAE-ProNet to SDM can help to use all functionalities of CAE-ProNet in SDM. However, team collaboration modules can benefit the most from information available in CAE-ProNet. As discussed in section 4.2.3, CAE-ProNet application can provide better transparency among various teams and dependency among them. It also provides optimized workflow which can helps team immensely to benefit from available information. Finally it results into better team collaboration.

Technical Specifications:

As described in figure 4.9 the flow between CAE-ProNet and SDM via an Interface. There are many possible ways to build the interface. E.g. Siemens" SDM (Teamcenter) can be coupled externally with CAE-ProNet using a Teamcenter standard way of PLMXML format. Data Exchange can be bidirectional or unidirectional. In above figure, SDM is considered as a black box i.e. without detailed functionalities as SDM features varies from company to company. The data required from SDM at a particular phase of CAE-ProNet are simulation quality reports, list of LCs, file structures and list of products, developments phases with respect to LCs. After processing in CAE-ProNet, it can export dependency library, LC specific dependency matrix and CAE-process.

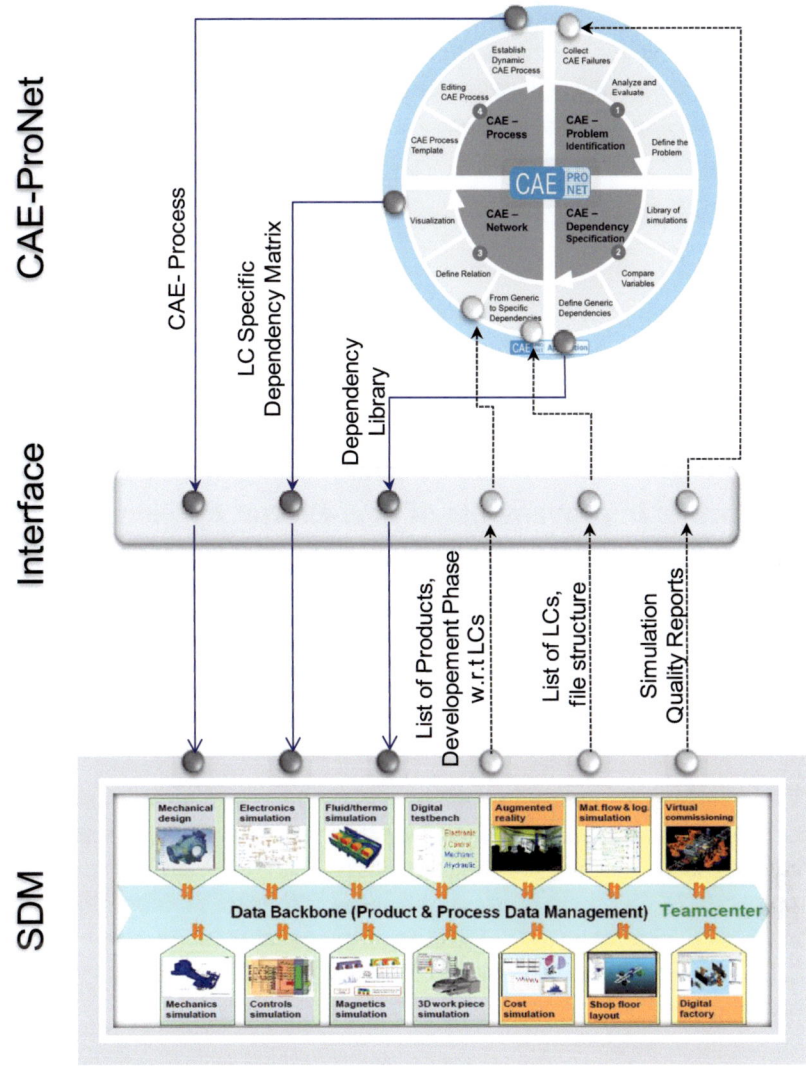

Figure 4. 9 Technical Specification of Interface between Siemens's
Team center SDM [Köpk-10] and CAE-ProNet

Benefits of integrating CAE-ProNet to SDM:

- It provides an opportunity for teams or workgroups which haven't explicitly implemented CAE-ProNet can still get limited benefits of CAE-ProNet.

- Existing information available in SDM is of course benefiting CAE-ProNet.

Statement 4.5: This section explains an accomplishment of objectives of integrating of CAE-ProNet to simulation data management. Using technical specification, CAE-ProNet methodology and application can be integrated in SDM and PLM.

4.3 Further Improvements of CAE-ProNet Application

New version of CAE-ProNet application can include dependency matrices of product to product and development phase to development phase as shown in figure 4.10. For example: For thermal analysis at car's underbody simulation various products plays a major role for underbody simulation. For thermal validation of steering shaft bellow, thermal inputs from engine, exhaust are required.

User Interface for library developer can be improved by increasing the number of basic formulas, which facilitates to highlight more theoretical dependencies. Indeed, the functionality of unit conversations exists but improvement helps to extend the area of field. A loose coupling between CAE-ProNet and SDM can be developed as described in figure 4.9 and additional enhancement can be through integrating CAE-ProNet internally in Simulation Data Management.

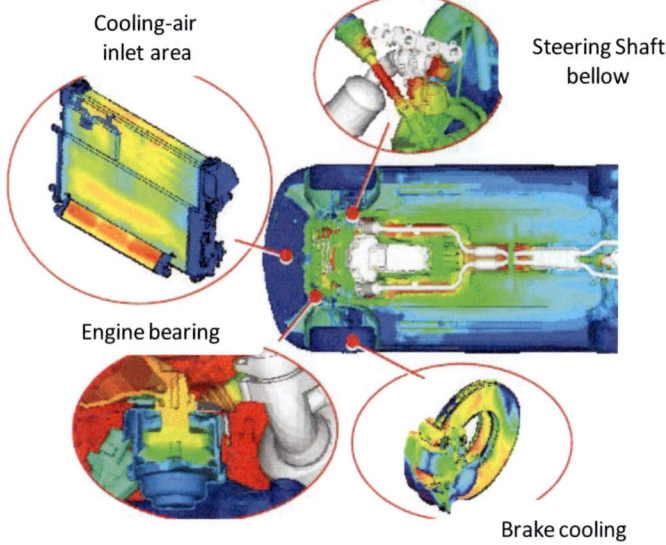

Cooling-air
inlet area

Steering Shaft
bellow

Engine bearing

Brake cooling

Figure 4. 10 Thermal analysis for Car's Underbody

4.4 Chapter Summary

This chapter described user interfaces that are implemented in this research work to verify the applicability of CAE-ProNet methodology. Existing methods and procedures that can be directly used are explored and investigated to accomplish requirements of CAE-ProNet. Hereby, objectives stated in chapter 3 are achieved and implemented. Objectives and statement are summarized in table 4.3. Objective 3.1.1 "System Analysis" is implemented and simultaneously verified in next chapter as statement 5. As further improvements of application a new version can be implemented with rest modules, described in section 4.3.

People and organization structure of CAE-ProNet (figure 4.1) is a big picture of the methodology. It describes the relation of CAE-ProNet with existing systems like data management, user groups and functional requirement. A closed loop work flow has been emphasized in this figure in section 4.1. Later on in section "Implementation of CAE-ProNet", user interfaces and GUIs of CAE-ProNet application are elaborated.

S.No	Objective	Status	Statement
1	Objective 3.1.1 – System Analysis	✓	Statement 5.1 (next chapter)
2	Objective 3.1.2 – Extracting Dependecies	✓	Statement 4.1
3	Objective 3.1.3 – Team Collaboration	✓	Statement 4.2
4	Objective 3.1.4 – Optimzing Existing Process	✓	Statement 4.3
5	Objective 3.1.5 – Integrating to Simulation Data Management	✓	Statement 4.5

Table 4. 3 Achieved Objectives

Four major interfaces are implemented and described via objectives, requirements, functionalities, benefits and further steps. First user interface is a method to develop library of simulations and dependencies which assists to identify dependencies automatically among simulations on theoretical bases. Implemented dependencies are summarized in table 4.2. Theoretical implementation of each simulation is given in Annex-C. Technical specifications are elaborated for an interface of CAE-ProNet to Simulation Data Management Systems. In next chapter, CAE-ProNet methodology is verified with an industrial use case using above implemented user interfaces.

5 VERIFICATION IN BUSINESS CASE

5.1 Introduction

5.1.1 Objectives

Verification, feasibility and practicability of the methodology are demonstrated in this chapter. The major objective of this chapter is to prove the applicability of this methodology using a business case in automotive industry. Amendments to implement it in existing business processes are illustrated. Simultaneously, verifying the feasibility and calculating the sustainability in this competitive automotive market are major goals of verification. Finally the expected benefits are certified using business case. CAE-ProNet application is also used to demonstrate and verify the methodology in existing business processes.

5.1.2 Verification Approach

Vast and diverse simulation field in automotive industry attracts to select a business case from automotive industry to verify the CAE ProNet methodology. An appropriate business case must have various simulation and load case conditions to validate its design. Existence of diverse simulation types like structural, fluid and mathematical simulations supports to build a sufficient CAE-Network to verify complexity of industrial application. Business case which consists of style, engineering design, cost and production requirements helps to verify team collaboration functionalities. Thereby, after evaluating various products from automotive Motorhood (also known as Car's Bonnet) is selected as business case for verification.

Define Motorhood or Bonnet: The hood or bonnet is the hinged cover over the engine of motor vehicles that allows access to the engine compartment for maintenance and repair. On passenger cars, a hood may be held down by a concealed latch.

Motorhood is used as a business case because of its diverse functionalities in safety, styling, durability, comfort and costing. That's why Crash, Aerodynamics, NVH, Stiffness, Fatigue, MBS and other simulation with large number of load cases are performed on motorhood. Therefore it helps to cover most of the simulation to build and verify CAE-ProNet. All phases and method-steps (described in chapter-3) are followed sequentially with a close eye on applicability in existing business processes.

Figure 5. 1 Isometric View of Mercedes Benz - Motorhood

5.2 Business Case: Automotive – "Motorhood"

Approach to authenticate the methodology is same as used while describing the methodology (as shown in figure 3.2) i.e. Problem Identification, Dependency specification, CAE Network and CAE Process. Durability workgroup which includes Stiffness and Fatigue simulation are used as target group for verification. Durability workgroup has a common feature of verifying the product design and its production validation for each and every condition. For example stiffness with respect to wind load, stiffness with respect to production, stiffness with respect to paint and drying process (as shown in figure). Thus selecting durability workgroup aids in considering various facets of simulation in automotive industry.

SI units are used to illustrate the business case. Cost factors are used in Euros. Foremost, the data is fictitious. The examples and data have no resemblances to any work group or manufacturer. Moreover, simulation and load cases are general automotive cases.

5.2.1 CAE - Problem Identification

Kickoff of methodology is by collecting the quality reports of durability workgroup. The durability workgroup includes stiffness and fatigue simulation and the workgroup is responsible for car's body-in-white, doors and Motorhood. Approximate number of load cases are 100 and 35% of them are dependent on other simulation. Table 5.1 shows a durability simulation quality report of Motorhood. Blue highlighted load cases are dependent on other simulation.

Model 20x			XYZ Org.					
LC No.	Simulation Load Case	Products	Development Phase	Quality Report Model 20x				
	Durability – All	Motorhood	Phase-2	200	202	203	207	209
1001	Durability – Longitudinal Bending	Motorhood	Phase-2					
1002	Durability – Side Bending left	Motorhood	Phase-2					
1003	Durability – Side Bending right	Motorhood	Phase-2					
1004	Durability – Torsion	Motorhood	Phase-2					
1005	Durability – Single Side Lift	Motorhood	Phase-2					
1006	Durability – Single Side Pull	Motorhood	Phase-2					
1007	Durability – Dynamic hit	Motorhood	Phase-2					

ID	Description	Component	Phase	1	2	3	4	5
1008	Durability – Front bending	Motorhood	Phase-2					
1009	Durability – Aerodynamic	Motorhood	Phase-2					
1100	Durability – Front hook	Motorhood	Phase-2					
1011	Durability – Max. Air Force	Motorhood	Phase-2					
1012	Durability – Cover buckling	Motorhood	Phase-2					
1013	Durability – Closing action	Motorhood	Phase-2					
1014	Durability – Transverse rigidity	Motorhood	Phase-2					
1015	Durability – Assembly Forces	Motorhood	Phase-2					
1016	Durability – Prefixing	Motorhood	Phase-2					
1017	Durability – KTL dryer	Motorhood	Phase-2					
1018	Durability – Bending empty weight	Motorhood	Phase-2					
1019	Durability – Fatigue	Motorhood	Phase-2					
1020	Durability – Edge Lift due to wind	Motorhood	Phase-2					

Table 5. 1 Durability Simulation Quality Report of 20x Model (Blue Highlighted are dependent load cases)

To validate the durability of motorhood these load cases are performed. From above table shows that 35 % (7/20) load cases are dependent. From simulation experts reviews the dependent simulation are performed using hardware prototype testing results or assumptions on the bases of previous results. Followings are some examples of current process.

Load Case 17: Durability – KTL Dryer

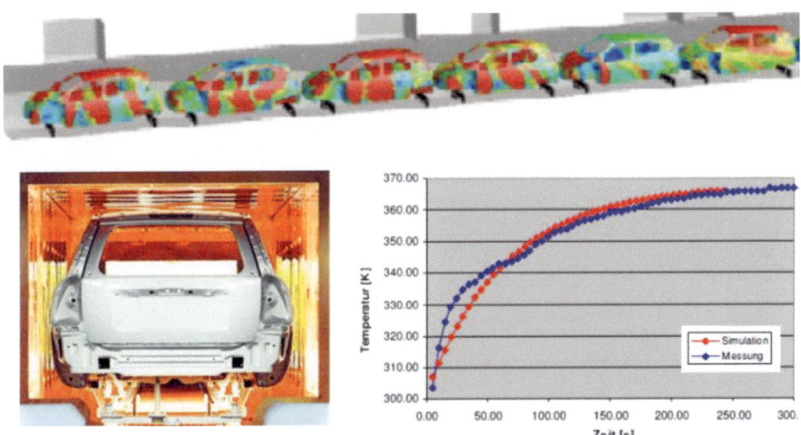

Figure 5. 2 KTL Dryer Process - CFD simulation (above), prototype testing (below left) and comparing simulation and prototype temperatures w.r.t time (below right)

To validate the design of motorhood in production process, various simulations are performed. One of them is KTL-Dryer. After painting process car's body undergoes in KTL dryer for 5 to 30 minutes depending on organization requirement. Temperature in dryer goes till 400 K (as shown in figure 5.2) to validate the design especially welding or gluing spots of motorhood, durability simulation for KTL dryer is executed.

To compute the durability simulation temperature distribution at car's body during drying process is required as input. In current process, temperature distribution is measured using hardware prototypes and used as an input for durability. On the other hand digital results of KTL-drying process is available but unable to use for durability. The quality improvement per simulation on each time step is 6%. Indeed simulation time is doubled but actual data is used.

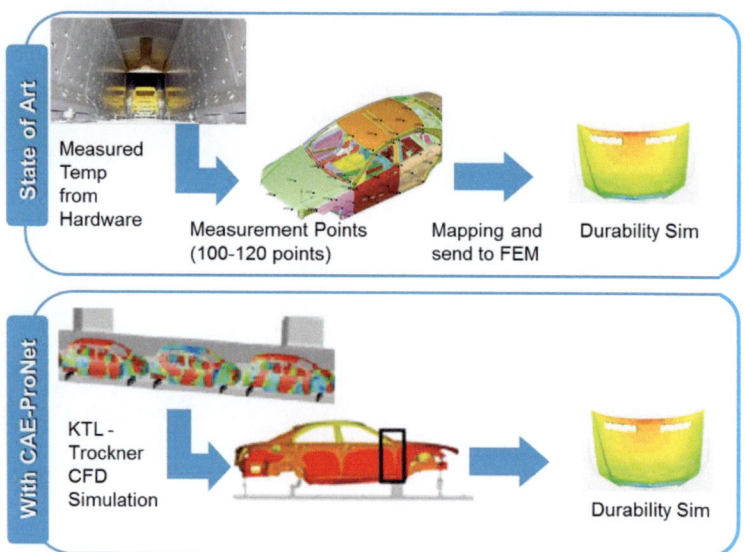

Figure 5. 3 Durability Simulation for motorhood – current
process (above), with CAE-proNet (below)

Load Case 20: Durability – Load Edge Lift due to Wind:

Another example of current process to validate motorhood design is by
applying simplified loads. For example in load case 20 of durability,
x KN force is applied on the edge of motorhood to verify durability due
to wind. Such simplified load cases are generated by personal expertise
or previous hardware prototype measurement results. However forces
due to wind are also available by aerodynamics simulation engineers in
same organization.

With current status, the load cases are based on hardware results and
simplified. These input results are used standard and may not be
accurate. The process uses various sensors and manual process which
affect the results on various products.

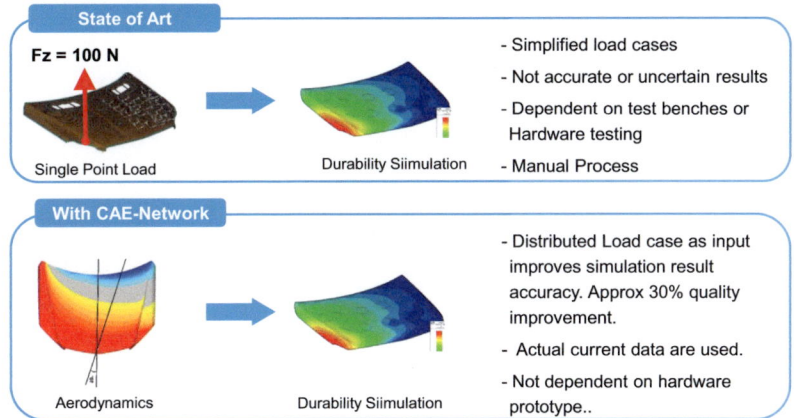

Figure 5. 5 Durability Simulation for motorhood – current
process (above), with CAE-proNet (below)

An additional example is given below in figure 5.5. The dynamics CFD
simulation is performed that is Acoustics simulation which helps to
optimized design to reduce noise due to wind.

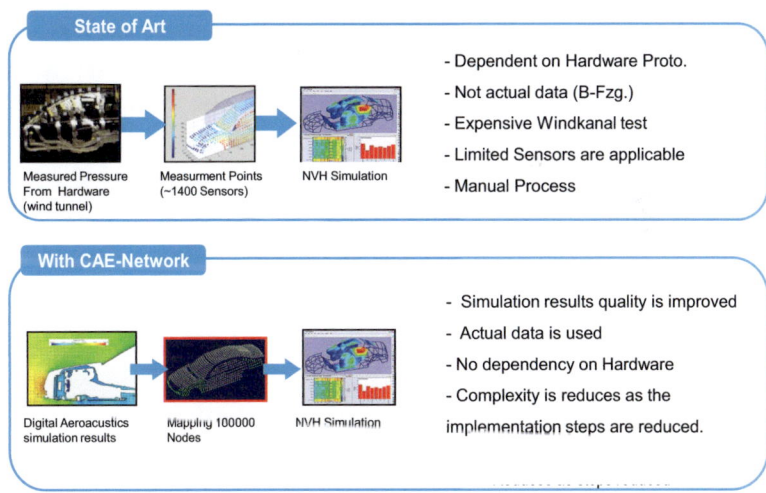

Figure 5. 4 Aeroacustics-NVH Simulation

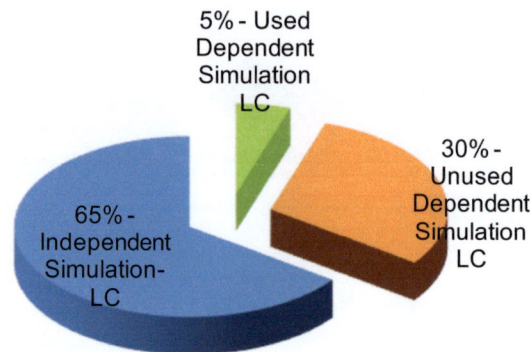

Figure 5. 6 Distribution of dependent and independent
simulation load cases

35% Load Cases shows the symptoms of simplified load cases, hardware prototype testing results and ignorance of relevant dependent inputs. Therefore more than $1/3^{rd}$ of the load cases can be improved thus shows high potential of implementation of CAE ProNet methodology.

Statement 5.1: Above analysis of simulation quality reports verifies the objective 3.1.1 "System Analysis" This confirms to check applicability of CAE-ProNet methodology for motorhood's durability validation system. It provides support to management decisions for the implementation of CAE-ProNet methodology.

Statement 5.2: Above load cases with CAE-Network verified the quality improvement. Three examples are elaborated in pervious section and one example is shown in section 2.2.1 figure 2.5 and 2.6.

Statement 5.3: Example Aeroacoustics-NVH verifies in reducing dependencies on hardware prototype and simultaneously reduces cost.

5.2.2 Dependency Specification

After decision takes by management on the implementation of CAE-ProNet on the bases on problem identification, dependency specification phase starts. In this phase, dependent simulations are identified. Dependency specifications are defined on the bases of existing simulation methods and tools used within the organization.

Taking into an account of implemented matrix from section 4.2.1 table 4.2, the verification for durability is performed. From the big dependent matrix, required simulations for durability i.e. stiffness and fatigue are selected as show in below figure.

As the matrix is build taking into the consideration of automotive industry, the same matrix can be considered for verification and requires no rework. For other organization, amendment may be required as simulation methods can be different as depending on the computing theory and tool used.

	Aeroacoustics	Aerodynamics	Stiffness	Fatigue	NVH	Multibody	Forming	Crash	Thermal	Electrical
Stiffness	Seq ↵	Pa	Seq ↵	Pa	*I*	Par ↯	Mo+Ma	Par ↯	Mod	Seq ↵	Pa	Seq ↵	Pa+Mo + Ma			Seq ↵	Pa	
	Yes	Pr	Yes	Pr		No	x	No	x	No	Pr+Fo	No	σ.			Yes	Tem	
Fatigue	Seq ↵	Pa	Seq ↵	Pa	Par ↯	Mo+Ma	*I*	Par ↯	Mo	Seq ↵	Pa	Seq ↵	Pa+Mo + Ma			Seq ↵	Pa	
	Yes	Pr	Yes	Pr	No	x		No	x	No	Pr+Fo	No	σ.			Yes	Tem	

Table 5. 2 Selecting Stiffness and Fatigue from implemented dependency matrix

5.2.3 CAE Network

List of simulations and dependencies for durability simulation are received from last section. All the products are enlisted and after selecting 06_Hood/Fender from the product tree, it filters the load cases that are taken place for hood. Similarly development phase and load case priority is selected to build particular cases for responsible load cases of above simulations. Below figure 5.7 shows the list of product in tree.

All load cases for a particular case i.e durability simulation workgroup, motorhood product, development phase-2 are enlisted in below figure. Organization of simulation tree is with Simulation type e.g. structural validation, than simulation (01_Stiffness) and at end load cases (01001_Biegung_hinterkante).

From Industrial view point, identifying dependent load cases is a major objective. Dependencies among simulations are already identifies and imported. In below figure, method engineer defines a computation method for load case "01015_Stiffness_Wind_270kmph". All the simulations and its load cases dependencies are highlighted as shown in bubble 2.

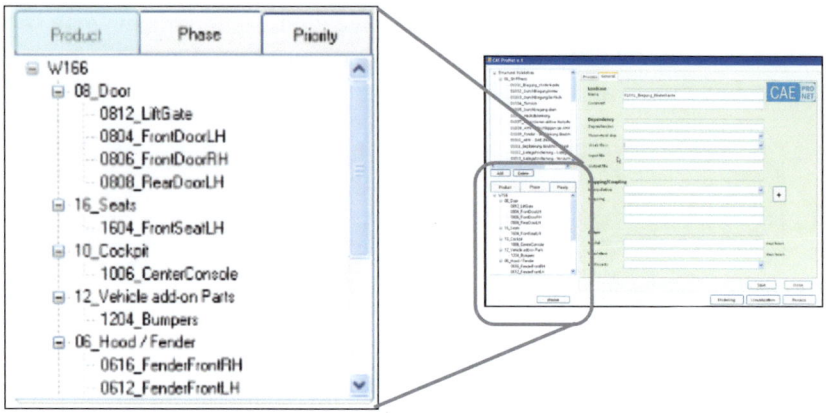

Figure 5. 7 CAE-ProNet application – Expanded Product Tree

Method engineer can select relevant dependent load case and define the relation using dependency, mapping and other parameters as shown in bubble 2, 3 and 4. If the same load case has more than one dependency, the same procedure can be followed to define the relations.

Statement 5.4: Above examples of customizing dependencies clearly depicted the flexibility of selecting dependencies. Moreover, transparency is improved as in shown in figure 5.8, 5.11 and 5.12.

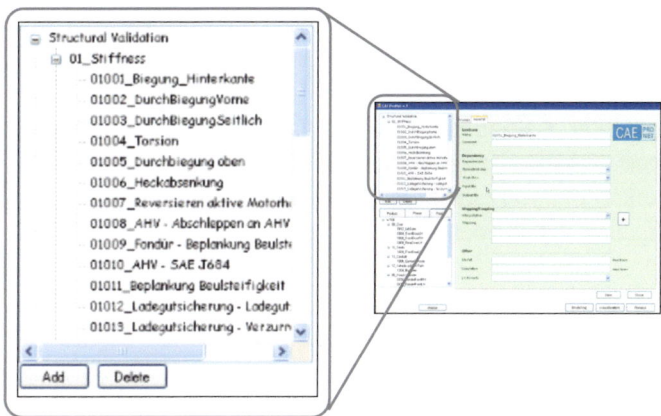

Figure 5. 8 CAE-ProNet application – Expanded Simulation Tree

Evaluation of Interpolation and Mapping Tools:

In phase 3 "CAE – Network" and step-2 define relation between simulation need interpolation method to perform mapping. In this section, interpolation methods are illustrated to select the required relevant interpolation method.

Definition: Interpolation is the procedure of estimating the value of properties at unsampled sites within the area covered by existing observations and in almost all cases the property must be interval or ratio scaled. [MaBu].

Difference between mapping and interpolation is minute and immaculate. Mapping is the process that transfers properties from one mesh to a different mesh, using a mathematical algorithm that approximates the transferred properties. This approximation is called "interpolation". The interpolation is a formula, or a system of formulas, that manage the way the properties are transferred from one mesh to the other mesh

Major requirement of evaluation is to find an optimal solution of interpolation for various simulations. We divide the simulation types in three parts 1) CFD 2) FEM and 3) Mathematical model (E.g Multi Body Simulation) simulation. Mapping in each relation requires optimal interpolation method. The interpolation method must comprehend the balance between interpolation time and quality. Because of this an evaluation of interpolation methods and mapping tools is performed and exemplified in this section.

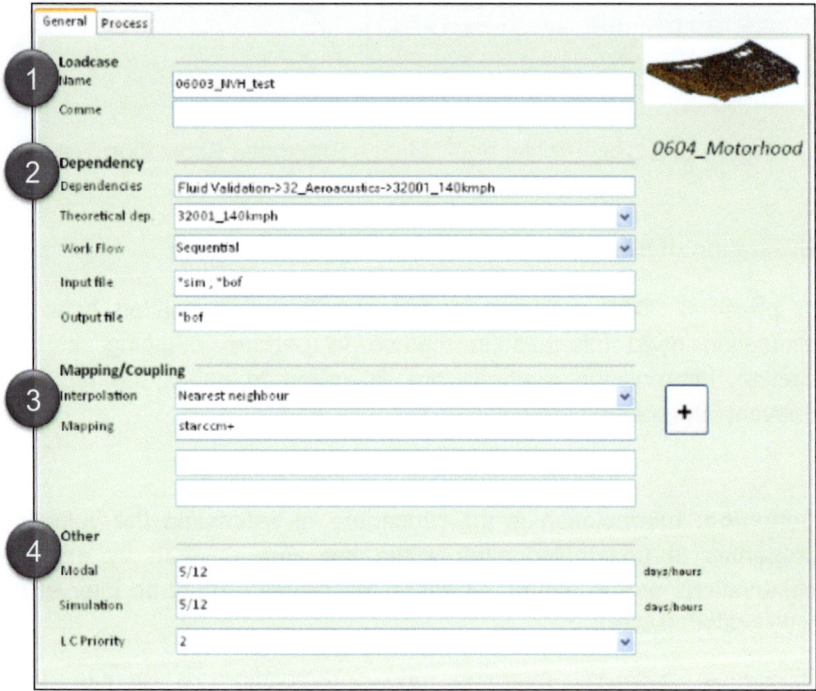

Figure 5. 9 CAE-ProNet application – Define Relation GUI

To test the accuracy, speed and memory consumption of the interpolation methods, the base example is CFD simulation performed in time domain with MATLAB (MATLAB – Technical Literature).

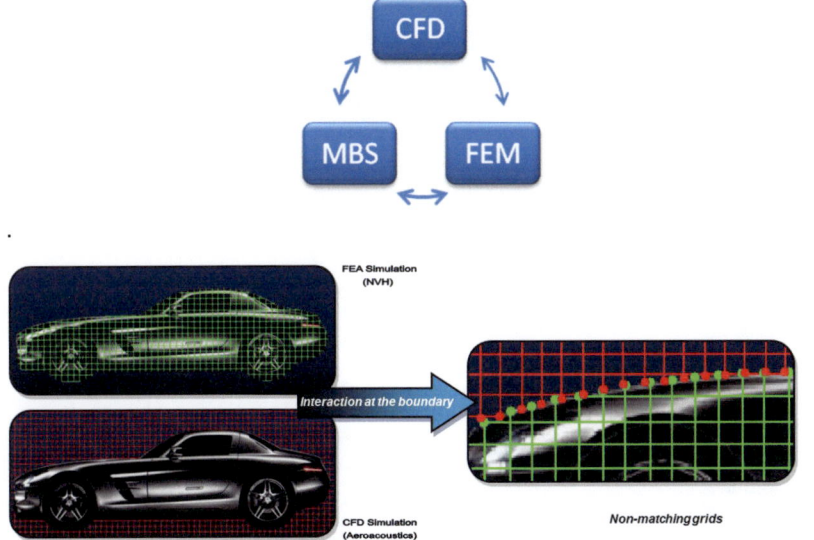

Figure 5. 10 Mapping Forms between CFD-FEM-MBS (above) and an example of FEM-CFD mapping

In order to have relevant results for interpolation comparison, the mapping has been realized from a coarse mesh to a fine mesh. During each transient interpolation, the time of processing (time needed to interpolate results and create FEA text files for each time step) is picked up. Moreover, the CPU capacity utilization is noted. The process to test the mapped results accuracy is the following table.

All the pressure given in the tables 4.1 are relative pressure, in relation to the atmosphere pressure. The average error concerns the whole transient mapping for the whole grid. The percentage of error is calculated by comparison with the real pressure average. The maximum error concerns the whole transient mapping for the whole grid.

Features			Accuracy		
Algorithm	CPU capacity utilization	Time for transient mapping	Average error	Maximum error	Percentage of average error
Nearest-neighbour interpolation	49000 Ko	2 min 00 s	0.646 Pa	12.65 Pa	12.78 %
Nearest-neighbour average interpolation	49500 Ko	3 min 03s	0.235 Pa	6.07 Pa	4.66 %
Inverse-distance weighting	52000 Ko	3 min 06 s	0.212 Pa	9.51 Pa	4.2 %
Linear interpolation	50500 Ko	3 min 42 s	0.112 Pa	2.03 Pa	2.37 %

Table 5. 3 Comparison of features for different interpolation methods: speed, memory consumption and accuracy

From this table, the CPU capacity utilization is not dramatically influenced by the interpolation algorithm used. However, the time for mapping is relevant. Indeed, the nearest-neighbor interpolation is the simplest interpolation, and the processing time is the shortest. On the other hand, the linear interpolation is more complicated, and the processing time is 85% longer. For real cases with millions of nodes and thousands of time steps, this feature can be a critical point.

Although the nearest-neighbor interpolation is short to process, its accuracy is not good compared to the other interpolation algorithms. The maximum error and the average error are relatively high. Such an error has probably a significant influence on the results in frequency domain (after the FFT). The nearest-neighbor average interpolation gives an average error under 5% and a maximum error about half of the nearest-neighbor interpolation. The time of processing is medium. The results of this interpolation depend on the radius parameter.

The inverse-distance weighting gives an average error under 5%, but the maximum error is critical, and can have a significant influence on the results in frequency domain (after the FFT).

Software Features		ANSA	MpCCI	Smart/Coupling	Star-CCM+
Supported software	Star-CCM+	OK	OK	OK	OK
	Nastran	OK	OK but limited (only a few properties can be mapped)	OK	OK
Cost		No extra charges: Daimler AG already gets licenses	6,300 euro/year with one FEA interface and one CFD interface (1050 euro for additional interface) • Purchase price: 18,900	•9,950 euro/year with one FEA interface and one CFD interface (700 euro for additional interface) • Purchase price: 29,850	No extra charges: Daimler AG already gets licenses
Other possible coupling or mapping		-	Thermomechanical coupling Electrothermal coupling …	Thermomechanical coupling Electrothermal coupling Electrostatic/Structural coupling …	Thermomechanical mapping
Interpolation algorithms		Polynomial interpolation (first order or second order, can be chosen by the user)	Shape function interpolation, Nearest Neighbour interpolation or Inverse Distance Weighting	Inverse Distance Weighting	Shape Function, polynomial interpolation (first or second order)
Transient process		In later releases	Only with the use of Ensight Gold as an intermediate tool	In later releases, but a customized macro can be created for the need	Not in the standard version, but a macro is being developed

Table 5. 4 Features of main commercial tools

The linear interpolation gives the best average error and maximum error. The maximum error is really low compared to the other interpolation methods. The small percentage of error is probably a crucial feature that leads to a mapped pressure distribution in frequency domain close to the real pressure distribution in frequency domain. However, the processing time is relatively long.

Statement 5.5: Outcomes of evolution are reduces the redundancy of interpolation methods and tools used in an organization. The evaluation leads to find out optimal solution to select interpolation methods and commercial tools. Nevertheless, it reduces the cost of development and improves CAE system by reducing the complexity.

			FEM — Stiffness						
			01009	01010	01011	01015	01017	01020	01023
CFD — Aerodynamics	31001		Seq Bif. Bof. / NI Sta. / 0 5 1	Seq Bif. Bof. / NI Sta. / 0 5 1	Seq Bif. Bof. / NI Sta. / 0 5 1			Seq Bif. Bof. / NI Sta. / 0 7 1	
	31002		Seq Bif. Bof. / NI Sta. / 0 5 1	Seq Bif. Bof. / NI Sta. / 0 5 1	Seq Bif. Bof. / NI Sta. / 0 5 1			Seq Bif. Bof. / NI Sta. / 0 7 1	
CFD — Thermal	10009						Seq Bif. Bof. / LI Sta. / 0 11 1		
	10008								Seq Bif. Bof. / LI Sta. / 0 5 1
FEM — Forming	13008		Seq Bif. Bof. / - - - / 0 5 2						
MISC — MBS	14008					Seq Bif. Bof. / NI Ma / 0 6 1			

Figure 5. 11 CAE-ProNet application – Relation Matrix of load cases

In further steps, similar evaluation can be accomplished to retrieve the specification for a tool which can perform multiple mappings i.e. CFD ↔ FEM, MBS ↔ FEM and CFD ↔ MBS in one platform. Open points are to evaluate interpolations methods for CFD-MKS. In practical, there are very less use cases where mapping of CFD-MBS is required.

The outcome of defining the relation can be viewed in the form of matrix. Load case "01005_Stiffness_Wind_270kmph" is dependent on Load case "31002_Aerodynamics_250 kmph". Other parameters to define the relation are filed in above figure. A screen shot of matrix to illustrate the dependency between described load cases is shown in below figure 5.11.

5.2.4 CAE Process

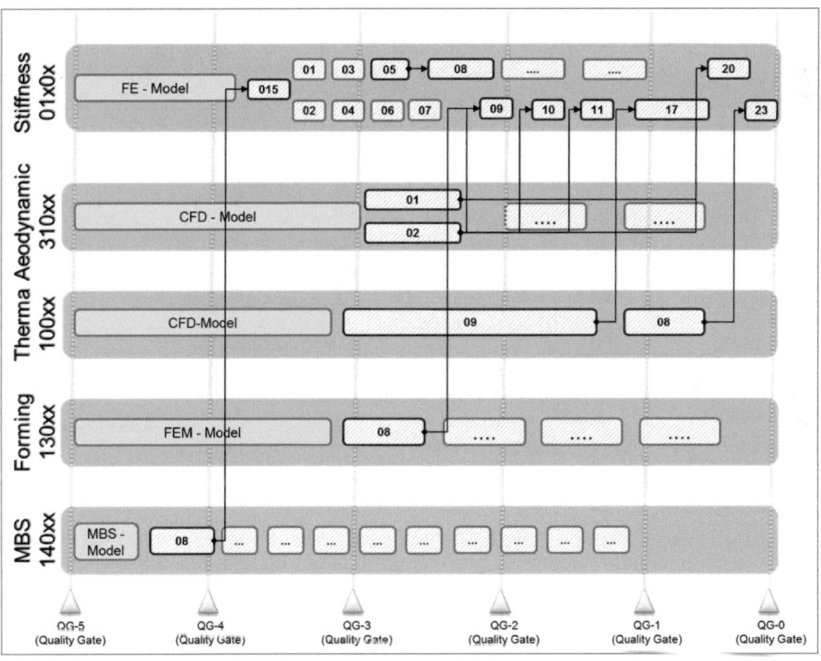

Figure 5. 12 CAE Process for motorhood in development phase-2

CAE Network for durability workgroup and motorhood is developed in last section. Using Design Structure Matrix (DSM) algorithm as described in section 3.2.4 is used to describe the CAE process. As time and priority factors are already stated in CAE Network thus it eliminates CAE Process template step. The final CAE process for motorhood for development phase-2 and till Load case priority level 2 is given in the figure 5.12.

After establishing the CAE Process in development system, responsible simulation engineers gets notification at each quality gate and before beginning of their Loadcase

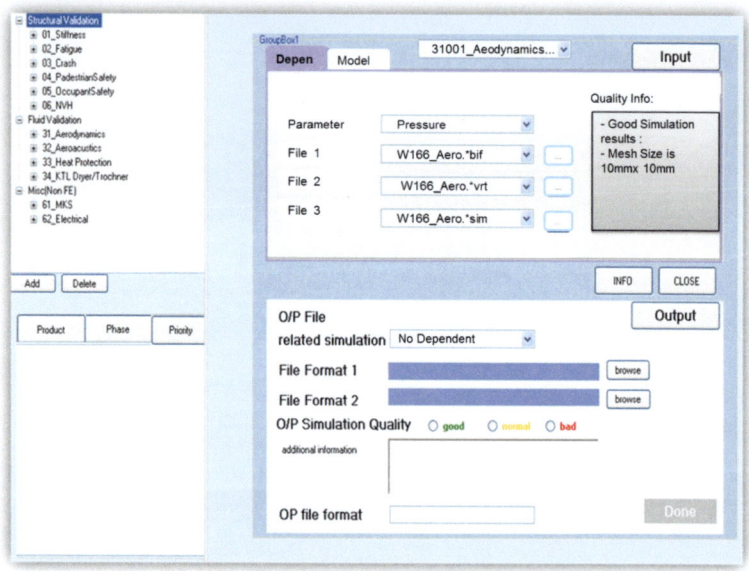

Figure 5. 13 CAE-ProNet Application Simulation Engineer GUI

For example, the load case "01009" responsible gets notification at QG-3 and after simulations results of LC-12008, LC-31001 and LC-31002 are saved in database. When the simulation engineer login in CAE-ProNet application, it shows all the dependent load cases and path of files saved in database. Using interface between CAE-ProNet and Simulation data management system, the data can be directly imported using CAE-ProNet simulation Engineer GUI as shown in below figure 5.13. After computing the load case, simulation engineer can save dependent data in Output. The quality of simulation output can be rated to inform the dependent engineer to ensure the quality of data that will be used in further load cases. The CAE process helps to meet the quality gates and transparency of quality improves system's transparency.

Statement 5.6: Facts of optimizing existing processes including CAE Process in the system are described and verified in this section. Expected benefits of better system organization by managing complexity of simulation dependencies and its process are demonstrated. It's also helps to use the actual existing data in the organization.

5.3 Business Case – Civil Structure

5.3.1 Objective

The objective of this section is to verify applicability of CAE-ProNet Methodology in civil structures where nowadays digital validation methods (FEM, CFD simulations) are common in use. It helps to model and calculate dynamic structural behavior. Thus, allow engineers to design and build civil structures in the most cost effective and safe manner. Simulations which are performed (as shown in below figure) and dependencies among them are highlighted in this chapter. Finally the expected benefits (from chapter 1) are verified using this business case.

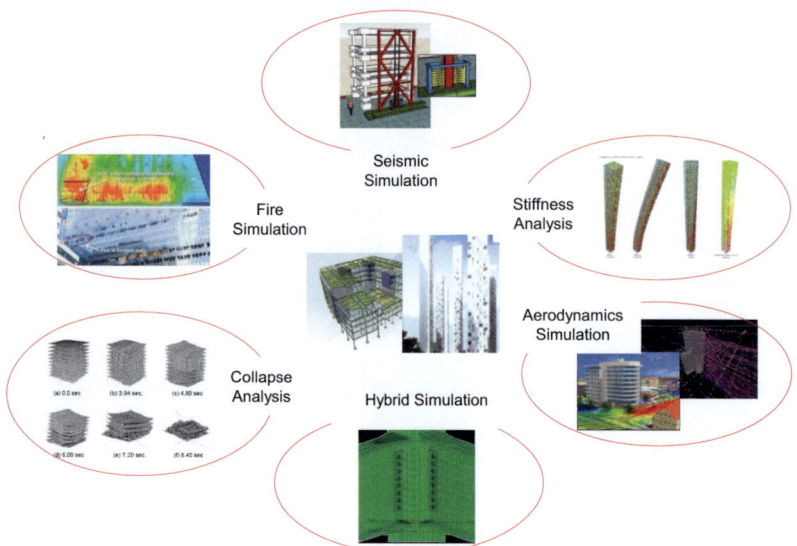

Figure 5.14 Types of Simulation for Civil Structures

5.3.2 Verification Approach

Major simulation which are used to design civil structures are Hybrid Simulation , Seismic simulation, aerodynamics simulations, impact simulation, fire simulation and blast simulation. There are severe blast loading supports that are designed and optimized by using FEM analysis. This helps to reduce expensive physical simulations of a specific explosive. This is known as collapse analysis and performed like a crash analysis in automotive industry. Seismic simulation undertakes devastating effects of earthquakes, structural response beyond the elastic range, including strength and stiffness deterioration. Quasi-static hybrid simulation is used to simulate substructures that primarily contribute stiffness and strength to a civil structure. Prevention of disasters due to strong winds and gusts are calculated by aerodynamics simulations. The dynamic characteristics of a structure - even measured at few points spatially on a structure - offer a great deal of information about the structural form. Consequently, the use of dynamic data for characterizing structural behavior has long been popular. All these examples are also linked to each other like Aerodynamics-Stiffness, Fire-Hybrid simulation, collapse-stiffness etc. As a result, CAE-ProNet methodology can also be executed in this industry. [CaZh-08] [WeXi-98] [PeNa-08] [LiXi-06] [SIMU-08] [KrCi-08]

A case-study of implementing CAE-ProNet methodology is explained using "The Burj Khalifa Project" which is a man made tallest structure in the world. The tower is 828 meters tall. Several simulations methods and load cases on Burj khalifa projects are illustrated and how CAE-ProNet methodology can be implemented in such projects are explained.

5.3.3 Executing CAE-ProNet Methodology

Aerodynamics structure and wind engineering played a major role on such massive structure. Thereby the simulations are early integrated in designing, where mitigating and enlightening the dynamic effect of wind was a major challenge. The dependency or affect of aerodynamics on its structure and foundation system helps to analyze the behaviors of the tower. Wind speed reach 160 km/hr at an altitude of over 700 meters in city centers and 55 m/s (198 km/hr) wind speed was implemented on wind tunnel models (1:500, 1:250 and 1:50 scale model). Thereby, the wind forces and the resulting motions in upper levels become dominating factors. Similarly in previous use case Motorhood, where aerodynamics simulation has a direct impact on durability of Motorhood. [Abde-10a] [Abde-10b] [BrPa-00] [Subr-10] [YaYa-12]

All 4 Phases of CAE-ProNet methodology are implemented in use case (Civil Structure).

Phase 1: CAE - Problem Identification

In this case study we consider Aerodynamics and stiffness analysis to evaluate the influence of wind on displacement. To compare the actual measured building movements to the predicted displacements, FEM structural analysis was done with actual material properties (concrete strength, modulus of elasticity, coefficient of thermal expansion, etc) and the foundation flexibility (subgrade modulus) as shown in below Figure. To calculate the foundation settlement, column strain effects, dynamic building characteristics and tower lateral displacement pressure on tower due to wind is required. This pressure change w.r.t time can be calculated by aerodynamics simulation. All above structural simulations have dependency on aerodynamics simulation which authenticates a need of CAE-ProNet methodology to identify the

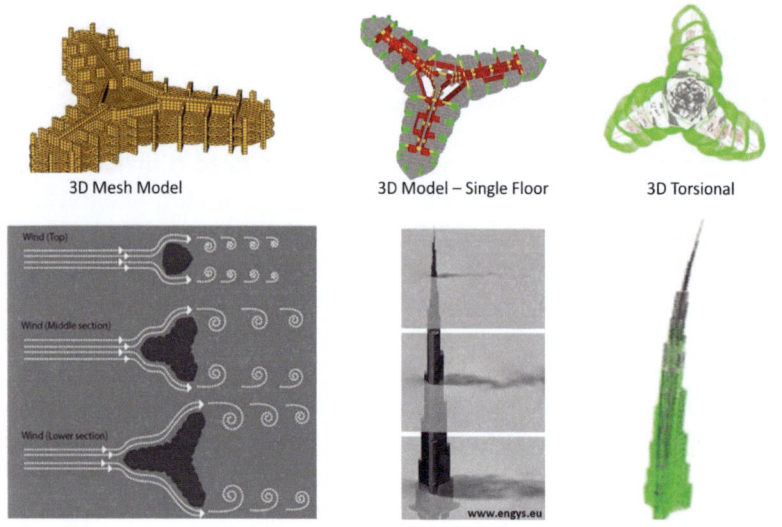

| 3D Mesh Model | 3D Model – Single Floor | 3D Torsional |

| Wind blow at different level | Aerodynamic Simulation | Lateral Stiffness Simulation |

dependencies among simulation and building a CAE Network.

Fig. 5.15   Several Simulation performed on Burj Kharifa [Jama-10][BaKo-08][Deat-12][Engy-10]

Phase 2: CAE - Dependency Specification

Considering the theoretical dependencies highlighted in chapter 4 table 4.2, stiffness analysis has a sequential relation with aerodynamics analysis. To calculate displacement of tower pressure distribution or stresses on tower w.r.t time are required. Pressure or stress are calculated by aerodynamics simulation and simultaneously various mapping methods have to be used to import the data in correct form.

Phase 3: CAE-Network

Several wind engineering techniques were implemented to control the dynamic response of the tower. To improve its dynamic behavior and preventing lock-in vibration multiple wind load cases were employed by disorganizing the vortex shedding formation (frequency and direction) along the building height. These multiple load cases vary with building shape along the height. The phenomenon is same as of automotives product base simulation and vehicle base simulation. Each floor is simulated and validated as well as whole tower. For maximum granularity the dependencies are linked with respect to simulation time which helps to build an effective CAE Process. Validating the aerodynamics shape is done changing the orientation of the tower in response to wind directionality, thus stiffening the structure normal to the worst wind direction. This can be calculated and verified by stiffness analysis using output of aerodynamic simulations. Dynamic responses of the tower have to calculate against wind excitation for construction time and after the construction. CAE Network matrix illustrates dependencies, mapping methods, time and process among each load case.

Phase 4: CAE-Process

To validate the maximum stiffness required normal to the worst wind direction continues optimization is required. Thus using the Design Structural Matrix (DSM) or CAE-ProNet Application, a CAE Process template can be build. In view of simulation time factor, number of load cases, development phases etc, the CAE process template can be edited and dynamics CAE Process can be established. This CAE process helps simulation engineers to use directly the output of dependent simulations and highlighting the influence at that particular development time.

This use case verifies the usability of CAE-ProNet methodology in other industries like civil structure where there is no serial production. Key advantage is to improve simulation result quality and bringing the results nearest to the reality. A product as well as whole system responsible engineers get a complete picture of dependencies among simulations and load cases. Another major advantage is system analysis, various wind load case can be integrated, thus help to figure out worst wind cases and its impact on structure.

5.4 Chapter Summary

This chapter describes the verification of CAE-ProNet methodology. Automotive industry and durability workgroup is considered as business case areas. Motorhood is used as business case for entire verification process. Because of vast and various functions of motorhood, enormous simulations are performed to validate the design of motorhood. It helps to validate the methodology in industrial point of view. Achieved expected advantages are accumulated in table 5.5.

S.No	Expected Advantages	Status	Statement
1	Section 1.3.1 – Enhancepement in CAE result quality	✓	Statement 5.2
2	Section 1.3.2 – Team collaboration	✓	Statement 5.3
3	Section 1.3.3 – Flexibility and Tranceparency	✓	Statement 5.4
4	Section 1.3.4 – Improved CAE System	✓	Statement 5.6
5	Section 1.3.5 – Reduced dependencies on Hardware Prototype	✓	Statement 5.3
4	Section 1.3.6 – Cost reduction	✓	Statement 5.3
5	Section 1.3.7 – Reducing redundant CAE and mapping tools	✓	Statement 5.5

Table 5. 5 Achieved Expected Advantages

Verification starts with identifying problems and challenges in simulations in durability workgroups. Approximately 30% load cases are identified as dependent and the load cases have uncertain results. This aids management to decide for execution of CAE-ProNet. Relevant simulations of durability workgroups are selected from the implemented dependency specification matrix. From practical viewpoint, CAE-Network and CAE Process are built and described using CAE-ProNet application.

Similar simulation workgroups can also be benefited using CAE-ProNet. Further areas of verification including biomedical science – artificial knee development, aerospace – wind development are elaborated in next chapter.

6 SUMMARY AND OUTLOOK

This chapter summarizes the thesis work and describes an outlook of this research work. Section 6.1 contains an outline and evaluation of vital results of the work. Section 6.2 illustrates an outlook focusing to the improvement of current work. Recommendations are elaborated for an enhancement of CAE-ProNet methodology, CAE-ProNet Application and possibilities of implementing CAE-ProNet methodology in other industries. Final wordings of the thesis work are collected in section 6.3 conclusion.

6.1 Summary

Now days, vehicle development time is approximately 2.5 – 5 years and development budget is approximately 500 to 2000 million Euros [KaAl-07]. To reduce vehicle development time automotive industry enhances digitalization, thus number of simulations and load cases are increasing exponentially. These increasing numbers directly affect quantity of dependencies among simulations which authenticate necessity of developing CAE-Network and CAE-Process. Addition to that, integrating them into Simulation Data Management is a vital requirement. The thesis work is solely focused on methods (stated in Chapter 1 as Objectives) to build CAE-Network, CAE-process and amalgamate them into Simulation Data Management. CAE-ProNet methodology approaches for an efficient and beneficial operation for CAE system in automotive industry.

Figure 6.1 illustrate the outcome of the research work. Currently, CAE Systems are without simulation data management (SDM) which leads to the deficiency of team collaboration between simulations. CAE Systems with SDM facilitate to save and retrieve data. Indeed it foster in team collaborations but simulation types are diverse and vast. Each simulation type uses different tool, file form and standards. It's a big challenge to link various simulations and executing an integrated process.

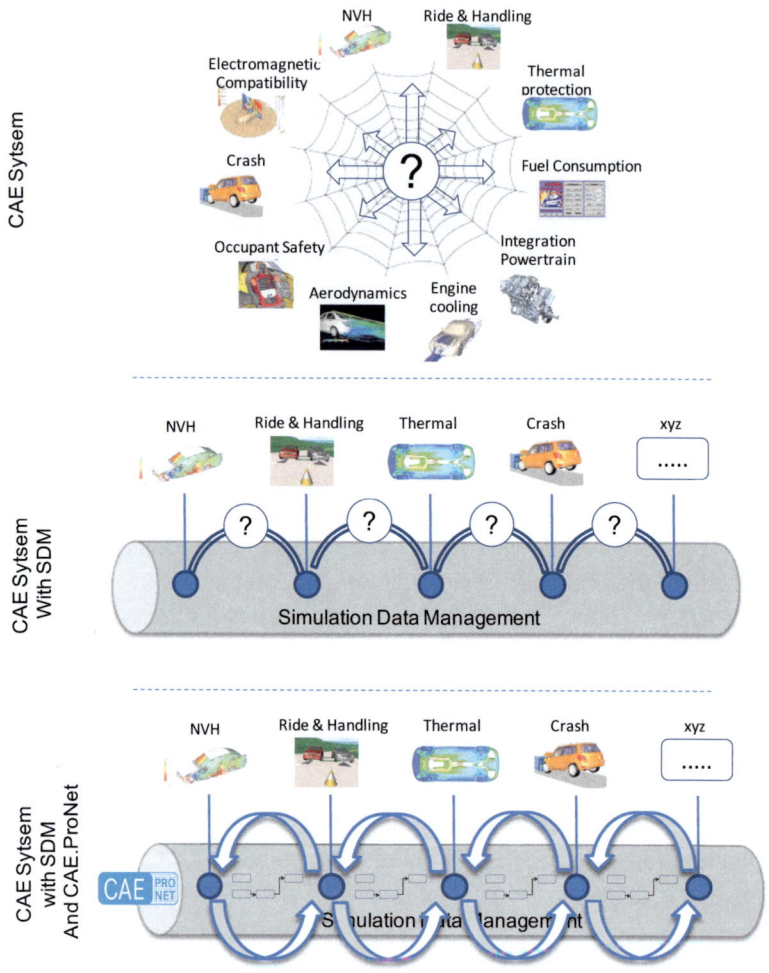

Figure 6. 1 CAE System with and without CAE-ProNet

Thesis outcome build a CAE Network which identifies simulation dependencies and link all possible simulations. CAE Process cultivates a sequence order with in simulations. Moreover, CAE-ProNet application is a cutting edge of this methodology. It helps users to understand and implement in organization.

Objectives and advantages are accumulated as major outcome of this thesis work and elaborated as follows:

6.1.1 Enhanced quality of CAE

A vital benefit of CAE-ProNet methodology for automotive manufacturer is improved quality of simulations results by receiving actual and detailed input data. The simulation results carried out using CAE Network are of better approximation and closer to real results. In section 2.2.1, benefits of CAE network are explained and an example is demonstrated in figure 2.4. More examples are used to verify using Motorhood as a Business use case in section 5.2.1. Identifying and analyzing failures due to dependent simplified load cases in vehicle validation phase reduces future failures.

6.1.2 Innovative method to identify CAE interdependencies

The method to identify dependencies among simulations is a core scientific added value. Developing CAE-Network and extracting dependencies using theoretical bases is an innovative aspect of CAE-ProNet methodology. Section 4.2.1 described the implementation of user interface for library developed which helps to build CAE-Network In section 5.2.3, outcome of CAE-network are explained. An implemented CAE-Network for Motorhood is given in figure 5.11.

6.1.3 Improved CAE system

Section "CAE – Problem Identification" aids in analyzing simulation quality reports. Thus, it provides support to management decisions for the implementation of CAE-ProNet methodology. Creating a common understanding of interpolation and mapping tools reduces redundant mapping tools. Section 4.2.3 verifies objective 3.1.4 "Optimizing existing process" by describing and establishing an optimized CAE process including interdependencies among simulation and their load cases in section 5.2.4. CAE-Process with higher granularity benefits managers for process understanding and controlling thus enhances CAE System.

6.1.4 Flexibility and Transparency

Benefits of reducing time of searching and collecting useful existing data are realized by simulation engineers. CAE-ProNet networks existing data and improves system transparency which leads to enhance effectiveness of simulation engineers as demonstrated in section 5.2.3 and 5.2.4. Flexibility to customize CAE-Network as well as CAE Process benefits vastly in OEMs. Possibility to add manually dependencies helps engineers to strengthen capabilities of CAE-ProNet methodology and application.

6.1.5 Fostered teams collaboration

System responsible get an overview about all relevant validations, dependencies, mapping and process related to the considered system. Thus, it benefits manufacturer by managing complexity of vast simulations and simultaneously foster teams' collaboration. CAE-ProNet application Figure 4.1, clearly depict the relation between method, process and simulation engineer. Immense potentials are realized and verified by the functionalities of CAE-ProNet application digital to collaborated teams and various users groups in section 5.2.2. An innovative way to manage and share the existing knowledge, experience and data in vehicle life cycle for the continuous improvement of product validation process.

6.1.6 Reduce dependency on Hardware

CAE-ProNet network assists dependent simulation to use the digital results of its dependent simulation. Thereby, it reduced the dependency on Hardware prototypes which is used to evaluate simplified load cases. As verified in section 5.2.1, it eliminates test rides that are performed for individual parts. Individual parts simulation can be performed using digital inputs as shown in figure 5.4. Reducing dependency affects in dipping development cost as elaborated in section 5.2.3.

6.1.7 Reduced redundant mapping tools

Mapping process is target as automatic process within CAE-ProNet methodology. This leads to have common mapping tools in CAE-ProNet and aftermath is a reduction of redundant mapping tools.

6.2 Outlook

6.2.1 CAE-ProNet methodology – Expansion:

Following recommendations are for the expansion and improvement of CAE-ProNet methodology. For the Section 3 .3 .1 – CAE Problem Identification (Area of focus – Expanding Simulation fields)

Indeed, the methodology is designed and developed to implement into mechanical structural simulations. But it can be extended and furnished with other disciplined too like Electrical, electronics, embedded System and mechatronic systems.

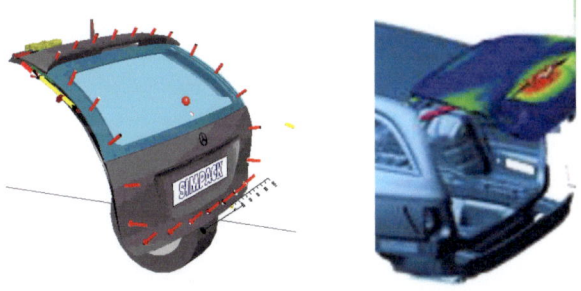

Figure 6. 2 Power Lift Gate System [OtBl-10]

For example: In power lift gate system simulation. Inputs are received from various suppliers. Each subsystem uses specific tool to validate their subsystem. Gas Spring subsystem uses AmaESim tool to validate their system, Gear System supplier uses modelica and Electric motors are validated in SimulationX. Later the complete system is built in Simpack to validate the kinematic system. This system can also be linked to stiffness analysis. As stiffness analysis is dependent on kinematics simulation for pressure or forces outcome during motion of lift gate

For the Section 3 .3 .2 – CAE Dependency Specification (Area of focus – Expanding Theoretical Relations). Theoretical relation within variables can be extended and adding relation among variable units enriches the methods to define dependencies.

6.2.2 CAE-ProNet Application – New Version

For the expansion and improvement of CAE-ProNet application, following recommendations are depicted. Referring to the Section 4.2.5 Interface of CAE-ProNet application to Simulation Data Management (focused to close coupling of CAE-ProNet Application with Simulation Data Management). Currently, CAE-ProNet application interface works as an external source. A close coupling or internally integrating CAE-ProNet in SDM will increases the functionalities of SDM as well as CAE-ProNet application. Simultaneously in enhances the stability of CAE-ProNet application.

6.2.3 Implementation in other industries

For the expansion and improvement of CAE-ProNet implementation, following recommendations with respect to individual industry are depicted. CAE-ProNet methodology can be adapted to other industries that use mass number of simulations to validate their system. More the number of simulation and load cases in that industry better the outcomes are.

Three major industries where CAE plays a key role and vastly used are taken as example. At first the Aerospace industry, which is the innovator and originator of CAE discipline. Some examples of simulation performed in aerospace industry for validation of "Wings" are collected. Dependencies among collected simulations are highlighted and suggestions to implement CAE-ProNet methodology in that industry are specified.

Medical science is growing industry and products are very delicate and sensitive. Number of simulations performed is not high as in automotive or aerospace but quality of simulation results plays a major role. Use case is Artificial Knee. Some simulations as examples are collected which are used to validate that particular knee and interdependencies are highlighted.

In civil industry mass of product is huge. Thereby simulation data and volume of outcome data is enormous. As similar to other industries, number of simulation performed are collected and suggestions to implement CAE-ProNet methodology are depicted.

Aerospace:

Aerospace industry has maximum number of simulation and load cases. Thereby, the requirement of networking methodologies is of high importance (as mentioned in Chaptar 1 Table 1.1). For the digital validation of aircraft wings, various simulations are performs like aerodynamics, durability, kinematics, multibody simulation etc. as shown in Figure 6.3. [AtHa-10] [HuKo-10] [WaGu-08] [FiPa-04]

Durability has interdependency with Aerodynamics as well as with Kinematic simulation. Multibody simulation requires outputs from Kinematics simulations and from hardware results. These dependencies are not with higher granularity level. Higher the granularity more number of dependencies can be identified. Electrical and mechatronic dependencies can also be integrated which increases the benefits. Therefore, CAE-ProNet methodology perfectly fits to build an efficient CAE Network and CAE Process for Aerospace industry.

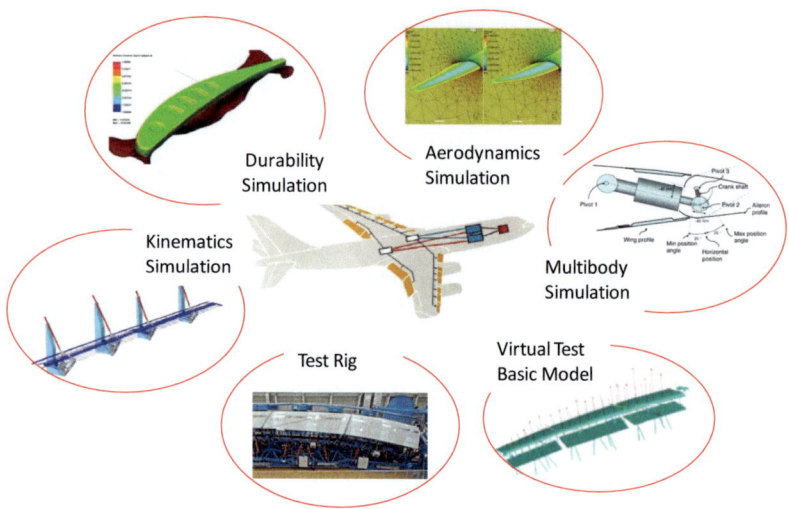

Figure 6. 3 Types of Simulation for Aircraft Wings

Medical Science:

This artificial knee is designed and developed to support patients who have problems with their knees. Total knee replacement (TKR) is a surgical procedure where worn, diseased, or damaged surfaces of a knee joint are removed and replaced with artificial surfaces.

An individual 3D model of knee is used for stress analysis. Microstructure FEM is used to determine bone stiffness and strength. Microstructure FEM also shows high potential to improve individual fracture risk prediction. Simultaneously kinematics, dynamics and drop test are performed using Multibody simulations. Blood circulation is also performed using fluid flow. [UcSh-01] [LIFE-12] [SmNe-10] [TeMi-07]

As quality of simulation plays a key role in such examples, thus each minor factor which has an influence is also very important. CAE-ProNet methodology helps to identify each and every single dependency. Consequently, CAE-ProNet methodology can be tailored and implemented in medical industry to validate efficiently artificial human systems like artificial knee.

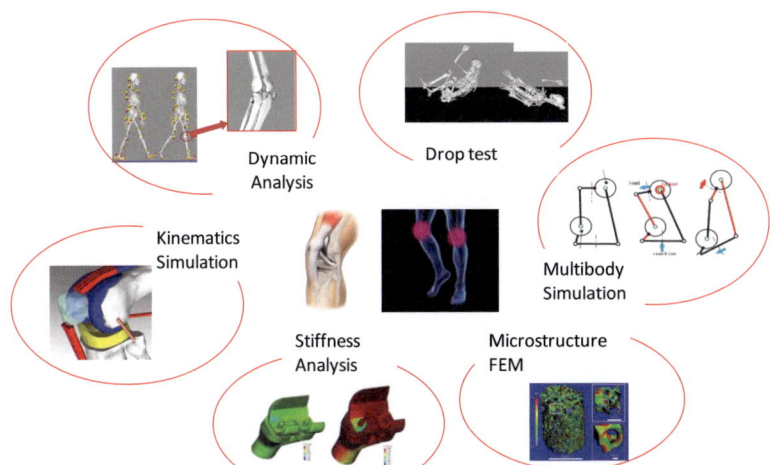

Figure 6. 4 Types of Simulation for Digital Validation Artificial Knee validation

6.3 Conclusion

Increasing customer demand and competitiveness in automotive industry drives all OEMs to be at first in innovation and new technologies. CAE field and holistic digital approach is comparatively new and growing. Companies are investing and exploring potential benefits of CAE. Therefore, CAE-ProNet methodology is making a valuable and significant involvement. The business case shows that CAE-ProNet methodology is feasible in automotive industry. The reimbursement of Implementing CAE-ProNet methodology are also far above the ground. Moreover, possibilities to apply CAE-ProNet methodology in other industries like aerospace and medical science are explained in outlook.

A Bibliography

[Alsa-11]   Ali M. Alsamhan. *"Rationale analysis of human artificial knee replacements"*. Journal of King Saud University – Engineering Sciences Saudi Arabia. Dec 2011

[Alat-11]   Risto Alatarvas *"Simulation models to determine health of skeletal System"*. Lappeenranta University of Technology (LUT), the University of Jyväskylä and the UKK Institute for Health Promotion Research. Article form Academy of Finland. 13th November 2011.

[Ansa-98]   ANSA Tutorial Beta-CAE System 1998.

[AnYa-07]   R. Anderl and Orkun Yaman. *"Integration von Hochleistungsrechnern im PLM-Umfeld"*. Fachgebiet Datenverarbeitung in der Konstruktion. TU Darmstadt. 2007

[Ausi-08a]   Autosim Consortium. "Current & Future Technologies in Automotive Engineering Simulation". NAFEMS 2008. 2008. 01-09.

[Ausi 08b]   Autosim Consortium. *"Current & Future Technologies in Automotive Engineering Simulation"*. NAFEMS 2008 White paper. Volume 6th. April 2008. 08-15.

[AUTOsim-08]   "Current and Future Technologies in Automotive Engineering Simulation (CAE) – Developed by the AUTOSIM Consortium" www.autosim.org, NAFEMS 2008.

[ArKr-05]   Silverstre Artiaga-Hahn, Nicolas Kruse, Frank Werner from Adam Opel AG *"Speeding up Aerodynamic Vehicle Development"*, Fluent News Summer 2005.]

[AtHa-10]   Ghassan M. Atmeh, Zeaid Hasan and Feras Darwish
              "*Design and Stress Analysis of a General Aviation
              Aircraft Wing*". COMSOL Conference Boston. 2010

[BaBo-09]   .Stefan Bauer, Jochen Boy et al. "*Automotive CAE
              Integration – Requirements and Evaluation of
              Interfaces*" Whitepaper Version 1.0 march 2010.

[BaBo-10]   Stefan Bauer, Jochen Boy et al. "*Automotive CAE
              Integration – Simulation Data Management*" Whitepaper
              Version 1.0 march 2010.

[Barn-79]   McCormick, Barnes W. "*Aerodynamics, Aeronautics,
              and Flight Mechanics*" New York: John Wiley & Sons,
              Inc. 1979.

[BaSr-96]   Milind A. Bakhle, Rakesh Srivastava, and Theo G.
              Keith, Jr. "*Development of an Aeroelastic Code Based
              on an Euler/Navier-Stokes Aerodynamic Solver*" NASA
              Technical Memorandum 107362. November 1996

[BeHe-05]   Ulrich Bestfleisch, Joachim Herbst and Manfred
              Reichert. "*Requirements for the Workflow-based
              Support of Release Management Processes in the
              Automotive Sector*". In: Proc. 12th European Concurrent
              Engineering Conference (ECEC'05), Toulouse, France,
              April 2005, pp. 130-134.

[BoBa-02]   Christophe Bogey, Christophe Bailly, and Daniel Juv'e.
              "*Computation of Flow Noise Using Source Terms in
              Linearized Euler's Equations*". AIAA JOURNAL Vol. 40,
              No. 2, February 2002

[Burk-04]   Mike Burkes "Toyota Motor Sales: Enabling Business
              Intelligence for Thousands of Analyst". Data Direct
              Technologies. 2004

[Brow-07]   Don Brown. "*Toyota Transformation*". Webinar and PLM
             Road Map 2007. 19th Sept 2007

[Cafo-09]   John A. Cafeo "*Industrial Perspective of V&V in
             Engineering Decisions*" IMAC 2009. Orlando, FL, USA.
             February, 2009

[CaZh-08]   CHEN Shi-cai , REN Ai-zhu , WANG Jing-feng , LU Xin-
             zheng "*Numerical Modeling Of Reinforced Concrete
             Slabs Subjected To Fire*" Department of Civil
             Engineering, Tsinghua University, Beijing 100084,
             China

[CHI-07]   WONG WAI CHI "Analysis of the suspension beam in
             accelerometer for stiffness constant and resonant
             frequency by using analytical and numerical
             investigation" University Malaysia. 2007. p 14-22.

[DaGa-12]   Gary Dagastine, "Numerical Simulation-Based topology
             Optimization Leads to Better Cooling of electronic
             Components in Toyota Hybrid vehicles". In COMSOL
             News – A mutiphysics simulation magazine Edition
             2012. Pp 4-7

[DeGe-10]   Deuring, Gerl , Dr Wilhelm "*Multi-Domain Vehicle
             Dynamics Simulation with Dymola*" VD Expo 2010 –
             22.06.10.

[DeLi-09]   Venkat Deshpande, Yeong Ching Lin and Martin
             McNamee. "*Streamlining the Automotive Powertrain
             Dynamic Analysis Process*". MSC.Software 2009 Virtual
             Product Development User Conference

[DiKo-97]   M. Diamaruya, H. Kobayashi and T. Nonaka "*Impact
             Tensile Strength and Fracture of Concrete*". J, PHYSIV
             FRANCE 7 (1997) Colloque C3, Supplement au Journal
             de Physique III d'aout 1997.

[ErDe-10]   Eric Dede, "*Inverse Methods, and Numeric*", COMSOL
              Users Conference, Session: Optimization, Toyota
              Research Institute of North America, Boston USA,
              October 8, 2010,

[EUCAR]   The   European   Council   for   Automotive   R&D
              http://www.eucar.be

[FaBe-10]   Bernd Fachbach. "*SPDM- From Overwhelming CAE
              Data to User Orientede CAE Framework for Full Vehicle
              Development*". NAFEMS European Conference on
              Simulation process and data management 2010.
              Frankfurt. Nov 2010.

[FiPa-04]   Guillaume Fillola, Marie-Claire Le Pape and Marc
              Montagnac "*Numerical Simulations Around Wing
              Control Surfaces*". 24th International Congress Of The
              Aeronautical Sciences 2004

[Flue-97]   Fluent 5 User's Guide Volume 1-4, Fluent Inc 1998

[Frit-10]   Peter Fritzson. "Functional Mockup Interface (FMI)" – A
              General Standard for Model Exchange and Simulator
              coupling". Linköping University. February 2011. P 5-7

[GoLa-10]   Lawrence S. Gould, "PLM for Simulation – A big payoff
              in CAE and simulation is in managing the data files with
              a system akin to PLM. CAE vendors have just the
              system" An article from Time Compression on   26th
              August 2010,

[Goud-08]   Lawrence S. Gould "PLM gets unified: basing PLM on a
              service-oriented architecture makes a "single source for
              the truth" possible, helps broaden the PLM "footprint,"
              and   brings   enterprises   closer   to   integrated
              manufacturing". Article   Automotive   Design   and
              Production. July 2008

[GüUw-01]   Uwe Gühl "Design und Realisierungeiner modularen
             Architektur   für   ein   Fahrzeugentwurfssystem".
             Dissertation by Uwe Gühl at Uni Stuttgart 2001.

[HoMI-06]   Marcel van den Hove, Bernd Mlekusch, "Automated
             process for occupant safety simulation" LS-Dyna
             Anwenderforum Robustheit/Optimierung 2, Ulm 2006

[HuKo-10]   Jun Hua, Fanmei Kong and Hugh H.T. Liu "Unsteady
             Thermodynamic CFD Simulations of Aircraft Wing Anti-
             Icing Operation" 2010

[IFF-10]   International Foundty Forum (IFF) "Future Development
             in   the   Automotive   Industryand   its   Markets".
             Management Engineers - Consultiung to Completion.
             Barcelona 10 Sept 2010

[ITEA2-12]   www.itea2.org/project/index/view/?project=217

[Jank-00]   Jeremy Ryan Jankowski. "The Basics Aerodynamics of
             Supersonic Flight" April 3, 2000

[JeBr-06]   Bruce   Jenkins   "Simulation   Data   Management:
             Rationalizing the Decision" Spar Point Research – Best
             Practice Series – Simulation DM 06062. June 2006. 01-
             10.

[JeBr-07]   Bruce Jenkins "Simulation Data Management: Business
             Drivers, Technical Enablers". Spar Point Research LLC.
             Danvers, Massachusetts, USA. 2007

[John-10]   John Day "BMW and MSC.Software plan joint portal
             development" John Day's Automotive Electronics news.
             March 2 2010.

[kaAl-07]   Alfred Katzenbach, "PLM at Daimler", Virtual Product
             Development Conference 2007

[KAn-01]   Andreas Kleber, "Simulation of Air Flow Around an Opel
              Astra Vehicle with Fluent", Journal Articles by Fluent
              Users JA132, 2001].

[Keln-10]   Ingo   Keutgen   .   "Nutzen,   Möglichkeiten   und
              Herausforderungen   eines   globalen,
              domänenübergreifenden   CAE   Datenmanagements".
              ProSTEP iViP Symposium 2010

[Kim-09]   Chul-Ho Kim "Governing Equations of Fluid Flow".
              Lecture Notes Seoul National University of Technology.
              2009

[KrCi-08]   Ted Krauthammer, and Jeff Cipolla University of Florida
              "Building Blast Simulation And Progressive Collapse
              Analysis" 3DS INSIGHT Jan-Feb 2008

[KrMa-02]   Krastel, Markus. 2002. "Integration multidisziplinärer
              Simulations- und Berechnungsmodelle in PDM-
              Systeme". S.I. : Shaker-Verlag, 2002. Dissertation, TU-
              Darmstadt.

[Kues-07]   M. Kuessner, "Realistic Simulation with ABAQUS",
              NAFEMS Seminar 28th – 29th March 2007, Wiesbaden
              Germany

[KuSh-12]   Rajeev Mohan Kukreja, S. K. Sharma and Ranjit Singh.
              "Collaborative simulation data management system".
              International J.of Multidispl.Research & Advcs. In
              Engg.(IJMRAE), ISSN 0975-7074, Vol. 4, No. I.
              January 2012, pp. 185-196.

[Kutz-02]   Myer Kutz "Handbook of materials selection". John
              Wiley & Sons Publication 2002. p 477-503

[LaGo-10]   Lawrence S. Gould, "Time Compression, Contributing
              Editor" August 2010.

[LaRa-11a]   Ralf Lamberti, "*Efffiziente Kreativität : Prozesse und methoden in der Automobilindustrie*", Lectures Karlsruhe Institut für Technologie (KIT), Summer Semester 2011.p17.

[LaRa-11b]   Ralf Lamberti, "*Efffiziente Kreativität : Prozesse und methoden in der Automobilindustrie*", Lectures Karlsruhe Institut für Technologie (KIT), Summer Semester 2011.

[Lifemodeler   www.lifemodeler.com/LM_Manual/modeling_analyze.sh
-11]   tml

[LiXi-06]   Ye Lieping, Lu Xinzheng, Ma Qianli, Wang Xunliu, Miao Zhiwei "*Seismic Nonlinear Analytical Models, Methods And Examples For Concrete Structures*". Department of Civil Engineering, Tsinghua University, Beijing. 2006

[LoSv-09]   Sebastian Lossau, Bob Svendsen. "Forming simulations based on parameters obtained in microstructural cold rolling simulations in comparison to conventional forming simulations ". 7th European LS Dyna Conference. Salzburg Austria. 14 May 2009

[MaBu-08]   Marian Bubal et.al. Computational Science – "*ICCS 2004. Proceeding Part 4*". 4th International Conference. Krakow, Poland. June 2004. 961

[MaSa-09]   Karina Malavazi, Juliana Paulino da Silva et al. "*The increasing Importance of Metadata*". T-System Median User Form. https://servicenet.t-systems.com/tsi/servlet/contentblob/servicenet.com/en/972250/blobBina ry /RelatedLinks_MEDINA_UF-cc-lo-1-ps-0.pdf

[Megu-87]   S. A. Meguid. "*Integrated Computer-Aided Design of Mechanical Systems*". ISBM 1-85166-021-6. Elsevier Applied Science Pub. Ltd. Essex. England 1987 p 7-12

[Mein-07]   Keith Meintjes "*CAE (Simulation) Data Management*"
               Technical Fellow – Global CAx Development and
               Integration 20th Sept. 2007

[Mend-09]   Jesus Mejia Mendoza. "*Design of Rear Cover
               transmission to support an existing and new vehicle
               programs.*" 2009 vehicle product development
               conference. Mexico 13th April 2009.

[Mill-09]   Mark Miller "Enterprise Development of SDM". 2009
               vehicle product development conference". USA 22th
               April 2004

[MIT-05]   Computational Methods for the Euler Equations.
               Lecture Notes Aerodynamics Fall 2011.
               (http://ocw.mit.edu/courses/   aeronautics-and-
               astronautics/16-100-aerodynamics-fall-2005   /lecture-
               notes/16100lectre47_cj.pdf)

[Modelisar-   Modelisar Project Profile – "Modelica – AUTOSAR
08]   Interoperability to support Vehicle Functional Mock-up"
               October 2008. www.modelisar.com

[Modelisar-   FMI PLM Interface – "Specification for Product Lifecycle
11]   Management (PLM) of modeling, simulation and
               validation information". Document Version 1.0 ITEA2 –
               07006. March 2011

[More-11]   Bruce Morey. "*Simulation Data Management emerges*".
               SAE International Organization. Automotive
               Engineering International. 17th May 2011

[MuDo-09]   Müller, Dominic "*Management datengetriebener
               Prozessstrukturen*" Phd thesis, Ulm University. 2009

[Muel-12]   Heiner Müllerschön "*CAx Data management*".
               Dynamore 2012. www.dynamore.de/en/it-solution/data.

[MuRe-08]   Müller, Dominic and Reichert, Manfred and Herbst,
             Joachim (2008) "A New Paradigm for the Enactment
             and Dynamic Adaptation of Data-driven Process
             Structures". 20th Int'l Conf. on Advanced Information
             Systems Engineering (CaiSE'08), Montpellier, France,
             LNCS 5074, Springer, pp. 48-63.

[NaJa-99]   Siva K. Nadarajah and Antony Jameson "A Comparison
             Of The Continuous And Discrete Adjoint Approach To
             Automatic   Aerodynamic   Optimization".   American
             Institute of Aeronautics and Astronautics AIAA-2000-
             0667. Stanford, California 94305 U.S.A. 1999.

[Nawo-   Alexa   Nawotki,   "Wege   zum   professionelle   CAE-
2009]   Datenmanagement" ,   Median   User   Forum   2009
             Stuttgart, May 2009"

[NeBi-09]   Frieder   Neukamm,   Markus   Feucht   (Daimler   AG),
             Manfred   Bischoff   (University   of   Stuttgart),   "On   the
             application of continuum Damage Model to Sheet Metal
             Forming Simulations". X International Conference on
             Computation Plasticity COMPLAS X, Barcelona Spain ,
             2009.

[NeFe-08]   Frieder Neukamm, Markus Feucht, et "A Generalized
             incremental Stress State Dependent Damage Model for
             Forming and Crashworthiness Simulation". Numisheet
             Conference, Interlaken Switzerland, 2008.

[NiSt-07]   Søren R. K. Nielsen, Jesper W. Stærdahl and Lars
             Andersen "Plate And Shell Theory". Aalborg University
             Department of Civil Engineering. Nov 2007.

[Nits-05]   Christian Nitschke "Outsourcing Vs. Insourcing in the
             Automotive Industry - The Role and concepts of
             suppliers." Master Thesis at University of Stellenbosch

Business School. p 47-52.

[Nish-11]   Vinesh V. Nishawala "A *study of large deflection of beams and plates*". Master thesis The State University of New Jersey. 2011

[Norr-10]   Marc Norris, "*The value of simulation process & data management – Lessons from a decade of production experience*" NAFEMS European Conference : Simulation Data and process management, Frankfurt 25.11.10

[OtBl-10]   Matrin Otter Torsten Blochwitz et.al. "Das Functional Mockup Interface zum Austausch Dynamischer Modelle". ASIM Worshop , 4-5 March 2012

[OvJa 04]   Ovtcharova, Jivka. "*Comprehensive Engineering Solution for Flexible Vehicle Manufactung*". COMPRESS frs Priority 1 & 2 joint call integrated project. 2005

[PeNa-08]   FENG Peng, HU Nan, HE Shui-tao, LU Xin-zheng, YE Lie-ping "*Collision test of a FRP pultruded box-girder for bridge structure*" .Department of Civil Engineering, Tsinghua University, Key Laboratory of Structural Engineering and Vibration of China Education Ministry, Beijing, China

[PiCh-95]   Piomelli, U. Chasnov, J. R., "*Large Eddy Simulations: Theory and Applications*", ERCOFTAC Summer School on Turbulence Modeling, Stockholm 1995

[RaBa-93]   Elizabeth M. Lee-Rausch and John T. Batina. "*Calculation Of Agard Wing 445.6 Flutter Using Navier-Stokes Aerodynamics*". AIAA 11th Applied Aerodynamics Conference Monterey, California August 9–11, 1993.

[RaCa-09]   N.R. Srinivasan Raghavan and John A. Cafeo. "Product
             Research: The Art and Science Behind Successful
             Product Launches" - ISBM 978-90-481-2859-4 Springer
             2009 p 115 -122

[RoAm-08]   Amy de Rauvray, ESI Group Press Relations *"Audi
             Works with ESI Group and HP to Advance Auto Safety
             Standards with Auto Industry's Fastest Supercomputer"*.
             ESI News release Paris France, ESIN FR0004110310.
             21st April 2009.(www.esi-group.com/corporate/news-
             media/press-releases))

[Royl-00]   David Roylance. Department of Materials Science and
             Engineering Massachusetts Institute of Technology
             "STRESSES IN BEAMS". Nov 21 2000.

[SaGh-11]   Atteshamuddin S. Sayyad and Yuwaraj M. Ghugal *"Flexure of
             Thick Beams using New Hyperbolic Shear Deformation
             Theory"*. INTERNATIONAL JOURNAL OF MECHANICS India
             Issue 3, Volume 5, 2011.

[Sama-08a]   Sama A. "Holistic Intention of Product, Process and
             Resources Integration in the Automotive Industry using
             the example of Car Body Design and Production". Th-
             Karlsruhe / KIT . 2008. 16-17

[Sand-11]   Karamjit Sandhu. *"Simulation of the Windscreen Defrost
             Performance"*- Star European User Conference 22-23
             March 2011.

[ScEl-03]   Michael Schlenkrich and Joern Elberfeld. *"Simulation
             Data Management – a corporate Initiative"*. EnDt –
             Engineering Data Grid. April 2003

[Schl-85]   E. G. Schlechtendahl"Evolutionary aspects of CAE
             systems - ENGINEERING WITH COMPUTERS".
             Spinger 1985 Volume 1, Number1 DOI:10.1007 /

BF01200334. Kernforschungs zentrum Karlsruhe 1985.

[Schl-10]   Michael Schlenkrich. *"Automotibe Solution: A cross-discipline focused Simulation Process and Data Management System for Automotive"*. NAFEMS Simulation Process and Data Management conference. Frankfurt. 25th Nov 2010.

[ScRa-11]   Alexander Schmid (IABG mbH), Andreas Raith (BMW AG), *"Multi-Body Simulation of Powertrain Acoustics in the Full Vehicle Development"*, Simpack User Meeting Salzburg 19.05.2011, 4-5.

[ScSt-10]   Stefan Schmid, *"Secure Your Simulation knowledge, Process and Data"*, NAFEMS European Conference: Simulation process and data management, Frankfurt 2010

[ScTh-10]   Wolfgand Schlüter, Carsten Tham *"BMW 2nd Generation Simulation Data Management- Experience, Infrastructure and Migration"*. NAFEMS European Conference: Simulation process and data management, Frankfurt 2010.

[SeLu-05]   Sergio Lujan-Mora. *"Data Warehouse Design with UML"*. University of Alicante. June 2005. 26

[SIMD-06]   "Data Grids for Process and Product Development using Numerical Simulation and Knowledge Discovery" Information Society Technologies Project No 511438.

[SimPDM-08]   Recommendation – "Integration of Simulation and computation in a PDM Environment (SimPDM)". PSI 4, Version 2.0. November 2008

[SIMU-08]   Simulia Insight Mangazine "Improving Bridge Performance with Finite Element Analysis Software".

3DS INSIGHT Jan-Feb 2008

[Söre-06]   Daniel   Sörensen   "*The   automotive   Development Process - A Real options Analysis*". Dissertation Universität Stuttgart, Stuttgart Germany. September 2006. p 2-10

[Smit-92]   Smith, H.C. "*The Illustrated Guide to Aerodynamics*". New York: Tab Books. 1992

[SmNe-10]   Smith-Nephew "Smith & Nephew Put New Knees through Their Paces with Realistic Simulation - Researchers study performance of replacement joints with Abaqus FEA". 3DS INSIGHT Sept-Oct 2010.

[SpBe-11]   Spickenreuther, Bersiner and Fricke "Realistic Driving Experience of New Vehicle Concepts on the BMW Ride Simulator using MBS Complete Vehicle Models" Simpack user meeting 2011. Salzburg. 18th May 2011.

[SpGS-94]   Spragle, G. S. & Smith, W. A, "*Hanging Node Adaption on Unstructured Grids*", Fluent Inc., Lebanon NH; AIAA 1994

[StBr-12]   André Stoffels (Audi AG) and Steven Bridgel (Microsoft) "*KPMG's Global Automotive Executive Survey 2012 - Managing growth while navigating uncharted routes*". KPMG's Global Automotive Executive Survey 2012 (Global version), Publication number 111218, January 2012.

[StFl-04]   Craig A. Steeves, Norman A. Fleck "Collapse mechanisms of sandwich beams with composite faces and a foam core, loaded in three-point bending. Part I: analytical models and minimum weight design". International Journal of Mechanical Sciences 46 (2004) 561 – 583. 2004.

[StHa-11]   Hannes   Stippel.   "Das   Virtuelle   Fahrzeug
             Forschungsgesellschaft mbh. CAE-Integration through
             Co-Simulation". Kompetenzzentrum

[SySu-11]   Gagan Syal, Nick-Ange Suyam-Welakwe und Vincent
             Tixier "*Technical Facets of a New Methodology to
             Describe Processes Contemplating Networking of
             Computer Aided Engineering Methods*".BUILDING
             INNOVATION PIPELINES THROUGH COMPUTER-
             AIDED INNOVATION IFIP Advances in Information and
             Communication Technology, Springerlink 2011.

[Tche-02]   Nadejda Tchertovskaia "Simulation model for the
             climate at the Windshield of a Passenger Car
             Compartment". Master Thesis Lulea Unioversity of
             Technology 2002.

[TeLo-07]   Lothar Teske, "*Virtual Vehicle Development Process at
             GM*". 1st Hyperworks Technology conference, Berlin
             October 23-24, 2007.

[TeMi-07]   Fumio Terauchi, Mitsunori Kubo and Hiroyuki Aoki "*An
             Artificial Knee Having A Five-Joint Multi-Link System
             Using Elastic Material*". International Association of
             societies of design research. The Hong Kong NIC
             University IASDR07. Nov 2007.

[Thom-98]   Stefan H Thomke "*Simulation, learning and R&D
             performance: Evidence from automotive development*".
             Harvard University, Graduate School of Business
             Administration, Boston, MA 02163, USA. 7th July 1998

[UcSh-01]   Uchida, Shibata, Zheng and Ito. "*An Adjustment Method
             of Visco-elastic Parameters for Above-Knee Prosthesis
             based on Mechanical Models*", Journal of the Society of
             Biomechanisms, Vol.25, No.2, 2001. pp.81-86

[VeKr-01]   Eduard Ventsel and Theodor Krauthammer "*Thin Plates and Shells - Theory, Analysis, and Applications*" The Pennsylvania State University, Pennsylvania.2001 (http://fte.edu.iq /eftrathya/46.pdf)

[Wald-96]   Chris Waldhart "*Analysis of Tow-Placed, Variable Stifness Laminates*". Master Thesis - Faculty of the Virginia Polytechnic Institute and State University. 1996

[WaGu-08]   Zheng Jie Wang, Shijun Guo And Wei Li "*Modeling,Simulation and Optimal Control for an Aircraft of Aileron-less Folding Wing*". WSEAS Transactions On Systems And Control ISSN: 1991-8763 869 Issue 10, Volume 3, October 2008.

[Wals-09]   Joe Walsh "*Bridging the simulation expertise chasm with intelligent automation*". 2009 Virtual Product Development conference Charkes Vill CA USA . 22nd April 2009

[Weig-04]   Annalisa L. Weigel "*MIT Aerodynamics Lecture*". 10 February 2004 (http://web.mit.edu/16.00/www/Aerodynamics.pdf)

[WeXi-98]   ZHANG Zheng-wei, SONG Er-xiang, LU Xin-zheng and CHEN Zhao-yuan "*Effects Of Concrete Masonry Walls On Structures Under Nuclear Blast Loadings*". Tsinghua University, Beijing.1998

[WiMi-09]   Harald Wilhelm Audi AG, Diego Minen "VI-Grade Virtual car model handling and ride bridging off and on-line simulations", Vehicle EXPO Stuttgart 2009.

[YaJi-04]   Xiu-Tian Yan, Cheng-Yu Jiang and Neal P.Juste. "Perspectives trom Europe and Asia on Engineering Designa dn Manufacturing". ISBM 1-4020-2211-5 (HB). Kluwer Academic Pub. Nederlands 2004. p 34-39

[ZeJo-12]   Dr. Josef Zehetner, *"CAE-Integration through Co-Simulation"*. http://vif.tugraz.at/en/products/icos/

Websites

[Audi-12]   www.audi.com

[BMW-12]   www.bmw.com

[Daim-12]   www.daimler.com

[Delo-11]   www.deloitte.com/in.

               Deloitte report "Driving Through BRIC Markets Lessons
               for Indian Car Manufacturers". Dec 2011

[MAI-10]   www.mai.org

               Malaysia   Automotive   Institute   "TRENDS   &
               CHALLENGES IN THE AUTOMOTIVE INDUSTRY -
               2010 REPORT".

[MSC-12]   www.mscsoftware.com

[PTC-12]   www.ptc.com

[SIMDAT-   www.SIMDAT.org
12]

[SCAI-06]   www.scai.fraunhofer.de "SIMDAT_brochure_2006"

B ANNEX CAE-ProNet APPLICATION

B.1 Use Case Diagram

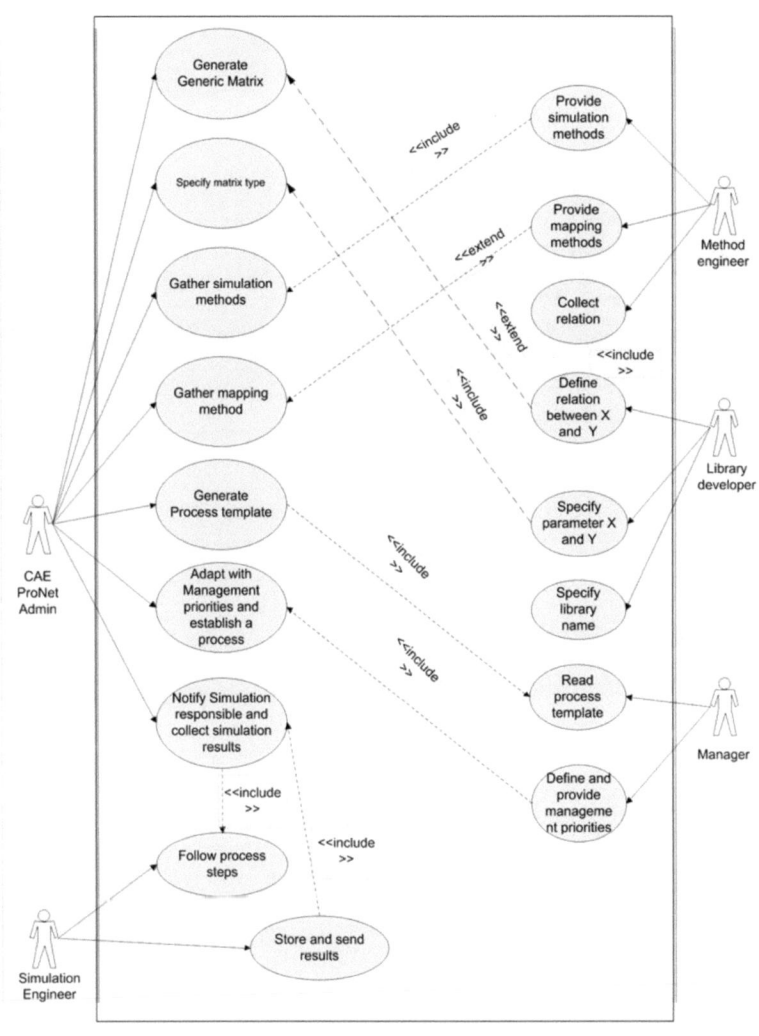

B.2 Sequence Diagram

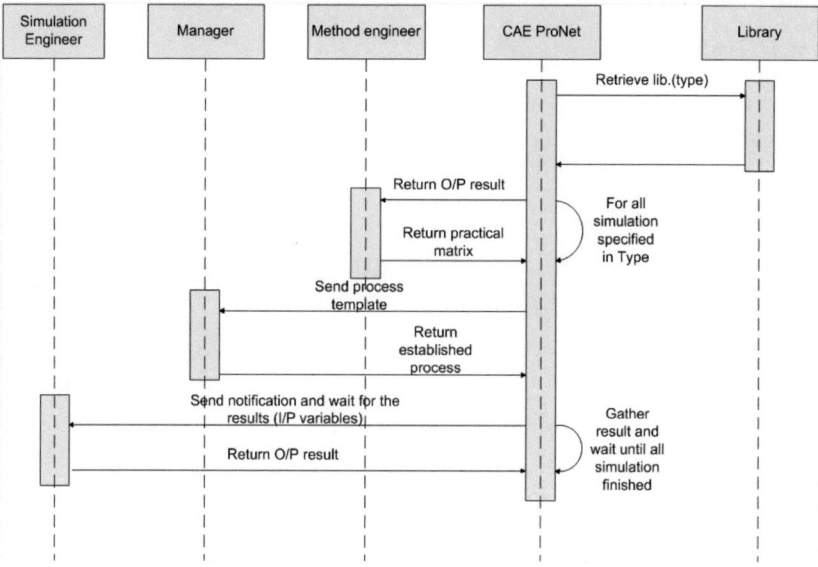

B.3 Activity Diagram

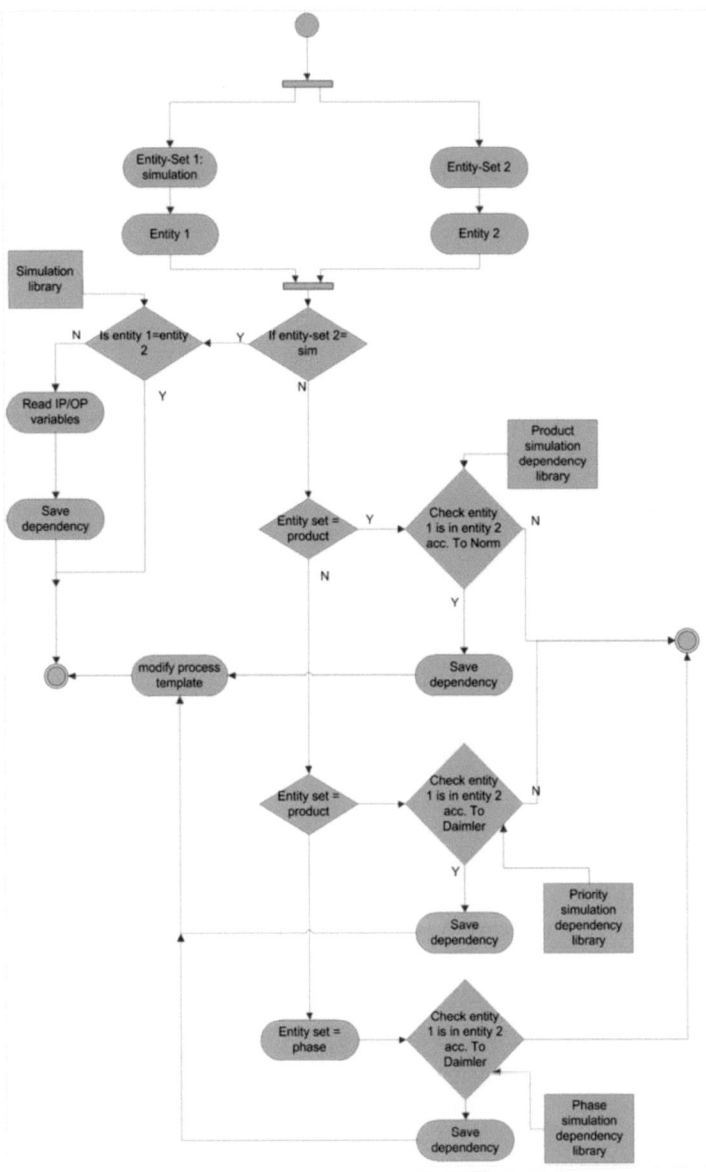

C ANNEX – CAE DEPENDENCIES

C.1 Aerodynamics and Stiffness

a) Aerodynamics

The equation used for Aerodynamic simulation depends on the assumptions made (compressibility, viscosity). The following equations concern a 2 dimensional problem (XY plane). The parameters are:

- P the pressure

- Vx the velocity in x-direction, Vy the velocity in y-direction

- ρ the density of the fluid

- μ the viscosity of the fluid

- gx the gravitational acceleration in x-direction, gy the gravitational acceleration in y-direction E = ρ.e + ½ (ρ.Vx2+ ρ.Vy2) the total energy per unit volume, e being the internal energy per unit mass

$$\begin{cases} \dfrac{\partial u}{\partial x} + \dfrac{\partial v}{\partial y} = 0 \\[2mm] -\dfrac{\partial P}{\partial x} = \rho.V_x.\dfrac{\partial V_x}{\partial x} + \rho.V_y.\dfrac{\partial V_x}{\partial y} - \mu.\dfrac{\partial^2 V_x}{\partial x^2} - \mu.\dfrac{\partial^2 V_x}{\partial y^2} + \rho.\dfrac{\partial V_x}{\partial t} - \rho.g_x \\[2mm] -\dfrac{\partial P}{\partial y} = \rho.V_x.\dfrac{\partial V_y}{\partial x} + \rho.V_y.\dfrac{\partial V_y}{\partial y} - \mu.\dfrac{\partial^2 V_y}{\partial x^2} - \mu.\dfrac{\partial^2 V_y}{\partial y^2} + \rho.\dfrac{\partial V_y}{\partial t} - \rho.g_y \end{cases}$$

Navier-Stokes (incompressible viscous fluid)

Navier-Stokes equations come from the three laws of conservation of fluid dynamics:

- equation of continuity

- conservation of momentum

- conservation of energy

Euler (in viscid compressible fluid)

$$
\begin{cases}
\dfrac{\partial \rho}{\partial t} + \dfrac{\partial (\rho.V_x)}{\partial x} + \dfrac{\partial (\rho.V_y)}{\partial y} = 0 \\[2ex]
\dfrac{\partial (\rho.V_x)}{\partial t} + \dfrac{\partial (P + \rho.V_x^2)}{\partial x} + \dfrac{\partial (\rho.V_x.V_y)}{\partial y} = 0 \\[2ex]
\dfrac{\partial (\rho.V_y)}{\partial t} + \dfrac{\partial (\rho.V_x.V_y)}{\partial x} + \dfrac{\partial (P + \rho.V_y^2)}{\partial y} = 0 \\[2ex]
\dfrac{\partial E}{\partial t} + \dfrac{\partial (V_x.(E + P))}{\partial x} + \dfrac{\partial (V_y.(E + P))}{\partial y} = 0
\end{cases}
$$

Bernoulli (inviscid compressible fluid)

$$
\frac{1}{2}.(V_x^2 + V_y^2) + g_y.y + \left(\frac{\gamma}{\gamma - 1}\right).\frac{P}{\rho} = cst
$$

For digital Aerodynamic simulation, an initial velocity input is applied. In addition, reference pressure and density (and often temperature) are given to specify the initial state of the fluid. The main output is the pressure distribution (in static) after the steady state is reached. As the pressure distribution is obtained depending on the evolution of fluid density and speed (and sometimes temperature), these parameters can also be studied as outputs.

Inputs:

-initial velocity applied on the model

-reference pressure (often atmosphere pressure for air flows) P

-reference temperature (often atmosphere temperature for air flows) T

-reference density of the fluid (often atmosphere density for air flows) ρ

-viscosity of the fluid μ

Reynolds number Re

Outputs:

- pressure or force distribution in the fluid domain (and consequently on the boundary with the moving object) P

-velocity of the fluid in steady state

-density of the fluid in steady state ρ

-temperature of the fluid in steady state T

b) Stiffness

Stiffness analysis can be performed using reference geometries formulas. But in practice, the structure geometries are too complex; the finite element method is used. The stress-strain relation is calculated for each element of the structure, and the matrices are assembled for a complete solution of the structure. The parameters of the following equations are:

$[\sigma]$ the stress tensor

$[\varepsilon]$ the deformation tensor

v the Poisson's coefficient

E the Young's modulus

G the shear modulus

ρ the density of the material

A the section area of the beam

Iz the second moment of area of the beam

l the length of the beam

α the coefficient of thermal expansion

T the temperature

Φy =   the shear-deformation parameter

Theory of beams

$$
\begin{Bmatrix} \sigma_{xx} \\ \sigma_{yy} \\ \sigma_{zz} \\ \sigma_{yz} \\ \sigma_{zx} \\ \sigma_{xy} \end{Bmatrix} =
\begin{bmatrix}
\dfrac{EA}{l} & & & & & \\
0 & \dfrac{12EI_z}{l^3(1+\Phi_y)} & & & \text{Symmetric} & \\
0 & \dfrac{6EI_z}{l^2(1+\Phi_y)} & \dfrac{(4+\Phi_y)EI_z}{l(1+\Phi_y)} & & & \\
\dfrac{-EA}{l} & 0 & 0 & \dfrac{EA}{l} & & \\
0 & \dfrac{-12EI_z}{l^3(1+\Phi_y)} & \dfrac{-6EI_z}{l^2(1+\Phi_y)} & 0 & \dfrac{12EI_z}{l^3(1+\Phi_y)} & \\
0 & \dfrac{6EI_z}{l^2(1+\Phi_y)} & \dfrac{(2-\Phi_y)EI_z}{l(1+\Phi_y)} & 0 & \dfrac{6EI_z}{l^2(1+\Phi_y)} & \dfrac{(4+\Phi_y)EI_z}{l(1+\Phi_y)}
\end{bmatrix}
\begin{Bmatrix} \varepsilon_{xx} \\ \varepsilon_{yy} \\ \varepsilon_{zz} \\ \varepsilon_{yz} \\ \varepsilon_{zx} \\ \varepsilon_{xy} \end{Bmatrix}
$$

Theory of plates and shells

$$
\begin{Bmatrix} \sigma_{xx} \\ \sigma_{yy} \\ \sigma_{zz} \end{Bmatrix} = \frac{E}{1-\upsilon^2} \cdot
\begin{bmatrix}
1 & \upsilon & 0 \\
\upsilon & 1 & 0 \\
0 & 0 & \dfrac{1-\upsilon}{2}
\end{bmatrix}
\begin{Bmatrix} \varepsilon_{xx} \\ \varepsilon_{yy} \\ \gamma_{xy} \end{Bmatrix}
$$

Generalized Hook's law

$$
\begin{Bmatrix} \sigma_{xx} \\ \sigma_{yy} \\ \sigma_{zz} \\ \sigma_{yz} \\ \sigma_{zx} \\ \sigma_{xy} \end{Bmatrix} = \frac{E}{(1+\upsilon)(1-2\upsilon)} \cdot
\begin{bmatrix}
1-\upsilon & \upsilon & \upsilon & 0 & 0 & 0 \\
\upsilon & 1-\upsilon & \upsilon & 0 & 0 & 0 \\
\upsilon & \upsilon & 1-\upsilon & 0 & 0 & 0 \\
0 & 0 & 0 & \dfrac{1-2\upsilon}{2} & 0 & 0 \\
0 & 0 & 0 & 0 & \dfrac{1-2\upsilon}{2} & 0 \\
0 & 0 & 0 & 0 & 0 & \dfrac{1-2\upsilon}{2}
\end{bmatrix}
\begin{Bmatrix} \varepsilon_{xx} \\ \varepsilon_{yy} \\ \varepsilon_{zz} \\ \varepsilon_{yz} \\ \varepsilon_{zx} \\ \varepsilon_{xy} \end{Bmatrix}
- \frac{E\alpha T}{1-2\upsilon}
\begin{Bmatrix} 1 \\ 1 \\ 1 \\ 0 \\ 0 \\ 0 \end{Bmatrix}
$$

For digital Stiffness simulation, load cases are applied. They can be punctual forces (in N), torques (in N.m), distributed pressure (in N.m2) or a combination of these load cases. Consequently, the input parameter is a force or a pressure (or both). Also, the material properties of the FEA model are provided: density, Young's modulus, Poisson's ratio, shear modulus, etc.

The output of Stiffness simulation is the displacement (or strain) of the structure. Depending on the requirements, the material properties and/or geometry are modified in order to guarantee a maximum displacement of structures.

Inputs:

-Stress $[\sigma]$ (or pressure distribution P)

-Young's modulus of the material E

-reference temperature T

-reference density of the material ρ

-Poisson's coefficient of the material v

-Shear modulus G

Outputs:

-Strain (or displacement) $[\varepsilon]$

c) Dependency

The dependency between Aerodynamic and Stiffness simulations is both dependency on model and data. First, the geometry of the structure has to be the same for both validation methods (dependency on model), even if the Aerodynamic simulation only needs the geometry of the outer surface to study the forces caused by the fluid. On the other hand, there is a dependency on data: **the pressure distribution** obtained thanks to the Aerodynamic simulation is used as inputs for Stiffness simulation, as stress input.

c.2 Aeroacoustics and NVH

a) Aeroacoustics

The equation used for Aeroacoustics simulation depends on the assumptions made (turbulences, internal stress, etc). Usually, the fluid viscosity is neglected and the effect of disturbances (in time domain) is predominant. The following equations concern a 2 dimensional problem (XY plane). The parameters are:

P the pressure

Vx the velocity in x-direction, Vy the velocity in y-direction

ρ the density of the fluid

C0 the speed of sound in air

σxy the internal shear stress due to viscosity

E = ρ.e + ½ (ρ.Vx2+ ρ.Vy2) the total energy per unit volume, e being the internal energy per unit mass

N the normal surface pointing towards the fluid

R the distance between a specified point on the surface and a specified point of the fluid

Lighthill (inhomogeneous wave equation)

$$\frac{\partial^2 \rho}{\partial t^2} - c_0^2 \nabla^2 \rho = \frac{\partial^2 (\rho.V_x.V_y - \sigma_{xy} + (P - c_0^2.\rho)\delta_{ij})}{\partial x \partial y}$$

Euler (inviscid compressible fluid)

$$\begin{cases} \dfrac{\partial \rho}{\partial t} + \dfrac{\partial (\rho.V_x)}{\partial x} + \dfrac{\partial (\rho.V_y)}{\partial y} = 0 \\[2mm] \dfrac{\partial (\rho.V_x)}{\partial t} + \dfrac{\partial (P + \rho.V_x^2)}{\partial x} + \dfrac{\partial (\rho.V_x.V_y)}{\partial y} = 0 \\[2mm] \dfrac{\partial (\rho.V_y)}{\partial t} + \dfrac{\partial (\rho.V_x.V_y)}{\partial x} + \dfrac{\partial (P + \rho.V_y^2)}{\partial y} = 0 \\[2mm] \dfrac{\partial E}{\partial t} + \dfrac{\partial (V_x.(E + P))}{\partial x} + \dfrac{\partial (V_y.(E + P))}{\partial y} = 0 \end{cases}$$

- Curle (taking into account effect of solid boundaries)

For digital Aeroacoustic simulation, an initial velocity input is applied. In addition, reference pressure and density (and often temperature) are given to specify the initial state of the fluid.

The main output is the pressure distribution (in dynamic) calculated for each time step of the transient simulation. As the pressure distribution is obtained depending on the evolution of fluid density and speed (and sometimes temperature), these parameters can also be studied as outputs.

Inputs:

-initial velocity applied on the model $\vec{v}$

-reference pressure (often atmosphere pressure for air flows) P

-reference density of the fluid (often atmosphere density for air flows) ρ

Outputs:

-pressure or force distribution in the fluid domain (and consequently on the boundary with the moving object) P

-velocity of the fluid in steady state $\vec{v}$

-density of the fluid in steady state ρ

-temperature of the fluid in steady state T

b) NVH

NVH analysis is performed using finite elements method. The pressure on the mesh in time domain leads to a displacement of the structure in time domain, and consequently vibrations. These vibrations are studied in frequency domain (after a Fast Fourier Transform is performed) and the critical frequencies and modes are isolated. The structure vibration leads to a change of pressure in the interior of the vehicle, according to the acoustic wave equation. From this pressure distribution in the environment, the sound pressure level can be calculated.

The parameters of the following equations are:

- P the pressure
- C0 the speed of sound
- ω the angular frequency
- ξ the particle displacement
- ρ the density of the gas
- Lp the sound pressure level

Pressure due to particle displacement

$$P = \rho.C_0.\omega.\xi$$

Sound Pressure Level

$$L_p = 10.\log_{10}\left(\frac{P^2}{P_{ref}^2}\right)$$

For NVH simulation, pressure loads are applied in time domain. The output of NVH simulation is the vibration of the structure and the resulting sound pressure level.

Inputs:

-Pressure distribution P(t)

Outputs:

-Modes of vibration and critical frequencies

-Sound Pressure Level Lp

c) Dependency

The dependency between Aeroacoustic and NVH simulations is both dependency on model and data. First, the geometry of the structure has to be the same for both validation methods (dependency on model), even if the Aeroacoustic simulation only needs the geometry of the outer surface to study the forces caused by the fluid. On the other hand, there is a dependency on data: **the pressure distribution** obtained thanks to the Aeroacoustic simulation is used as inputs for NVH simulation.

C.3 Crash and Forming

a) Forming

Forming simulation is performed using finite elements method. The strength and displacement are determined depending on the forming process: load cases, temperature, etc. The main parameters involved in forming simulation are (depending on the forming process):

- T the temperature of forming
- υ12 the Poisson ratio
- G12 the shear modulus
- E1 the modulus of elasticity along the fiber
- E2 the modulus of elasticity transverse to the fiber
- $[\sigma]$ the stress tensor
- $[\varepsilon]$ the deformation tensor
- ρ the density of the material
- α the coefficient of thermal expansion

Plies' rigidities (laminate calculation)

$$[Q]_k = \begin{bmatrix} Q_{11} & Q_{12} & 0 \\ Q_{21} & Q_{22} & 0 \\ 0 & 0 & Q_{33} \end{bmatrix} = \begin{bmatrix} \dfrac{E_1}{1-\upsilon_{12}^2.\dfrac{E_2}{E_1}} & \dfrac{\upsilon_{12}.E_1}{1-\upsilon_{12}^2.\dfrac{E_2}{E_1}} & 0 \\ \dfrac{\upsilon_{12}.E_1}{1-\upsilon_{12}^2.\dfrac{E_2}{E_1}} & \dfrac{E_1}{1-\upsilon_{12}^2.\dfrac{E_2}{E_1}} & 0 \\ 0 & 0 & G_{12} \end{bmatrix}$$

For digital Forming simulation, forming load cases are applied. They can be punctual forces (in N), torques (in N.m), distributed pressure (in N.m2) or a combination of these load cases. Consequently, the input parameter is a force or a pressure (or both). Also, the initial material properties of the FEA model are provided: density, Young's modulus, Poisson ratio, shear modulus, etc.

The output of Stiffness simulation is the displacement (or strain) of the structure, as well as the new material properties: density, Young's modulus, Poisson ratio, shear modulus, coefficient of thermal expansion, etc.

Inputs:

-Strain $[\varepsilon]$

-Young's modulus of the material E

-reference temperature T

-reference density of the material ρ

Poisson's coefficient of the material ν

Shear modulus G

Coefficient of thermal expansion αT

Outputs:

Stress $[\sigma]$

Young's modulus of the material E

temperature T

density of the material ρ

Poisson's coefficient of the material v

Shear modulus G

Coefficient of thermal expansion αT

b) Crash

Crash analysis is a transient simulation performed using finite elements method. Depending on the mass and speed of the vehicle, the kinetic energy is calculated. Assuming that this kinetic energy is the average work needed to stop the car multiplied by the distance needed to stop the car, the force load case applied on the car is calculated for each time step. From the stress tensor, the deformation can be calculated using usual stiffness algorithm. The distance needed to stop the car is calculated thanks to the norms in terms of maximal acceleration that can handle passengers. The length of time steps is calculated in relation to the deformation of the structure, consequently depending on the material properties. The parameters of the following equations are:

- $[\sigma]$ the stress tensor
- $[\varepsilon]$ the deformation tensor
- v the Poisson's coefficient
- E the Young's modulus
- ρ the density of the material
- M the mass of the vehicle
- V the speed of the vehicle

- d the distance needed to stop the vehicle

- Favg the average force applied on the vehicle during a small period of time

- ΔTel the elementary time step (in s)

Conservation of energy of the vehicle

$$F_{avg}.d = -\frac{1}{2}.M.V^2$$

Time step calculation

$$\Delta T_{el} = \frac{characteristic\ size}{\sqrt{\dfrac{\lambda + 2\mu}{\rho}}}$$

where

$$characteristic\ size = \frac{volume\,(of\ element)}{\max\,(facets\ area)}$$

$$\lambda = \frac{E\,v}{(1+v)(1-2v)} \quad and \quad \mu = \frac{E}{2(1+v)}$$

Strain calculation (for one time step)

$$\begin{Bmatrix} \sigma_{xx} \\ \sigma_{yy} \\ \sigma_{zz} \\ \sigma_{yz} \\ \sigma_{zx} \\ \sigma_{xy} \end{Bmatrix} = \frac{E}{(1+\upsilon)(1-2\upsilon)} \cdot \begin{bmatrix} 1-\upsilon & \upsilon & \upsilon & 0 & 0 & 0 \\ \upsilon & 1-\upsilon & \upsilon & 0 & 0 & 0 \\ \upsilon & \upsilon & 1-\upsilon & 0 & 0 & 0 \\ 0 & 0 & 0 & \dfrac{1-2\upsilon}{2} & 0 & 0 \\ 0 & 0 & 0 & 0 & \dfrac{1-2\upsilon}{2} & 0 \\ 0 & 0 & 0 & 0 & 0 & \dfrac{1-2\upsilon}{2} \end{bmatrix} \begin{Bmatrix} \varepsilon_{xx} \\ \varepsilon_{yy} \\ \varepsilon_{zz} \\ \varepsilon_{yz} \\ \varepsilon_{zx} \\ \varepsilon_{xy} \end{Bmatrix}$$

For digital Crash simulation, an initial speed of the vehicle is applied. The mass of the car is also needed to calculate the force distribution at each time step of the simulation. Also, in order to calculate the structure deformation and the elementary time step, the material properties of the FEA model are provided: density, Young's modulus, Poisson's ratio, shear modulus, etc.

The output of Crash simulation is the deformation of the structure. The vehicle displacement can also be studied. Depending on the requirements, the material properties and/or geometry are modified in order to guarantee a maximum displacement of structures.

Inputs:

- Young's modulus of the material E

- reference density of the material ρ

- Poisson's coefficient of the material ν

- Shear modulus G

- Vehicle mass M

- Vehicle velocity V

Outputs:

- Strain (or displacement) $[\varepsilon]$

c) Dependency

The dependency between Forming and Crash simulations is dependency on model. **First, the model geometry obtained after forming simulation is used in crash simulation** (the initial CAD model can be different in thickness for example). On the other hand, the material properties are modified after forming simulation (compared to initial CAD model which contains classical material properties).

c.4 Multibody Simulation and Fatigue Simulation

a) Multibody simulation.

Depending on the mass and speed of the vehicle, the kinetic energy is calculated. Assuming that this kinetic energy is the average work needed to stop the car multiplied by the distance needed to stop the car, the force load case applied on the car is calculated for each time step. From the stress tensor, the deformation can be calculated using usual stiffness algorithm. The distance needed to stop the car is calculated thanks to the norms in terms of maximal acceleration that can handle passengers. The length of time steps is calculated in relation to the deformation of the structure, consequently depending on the material properties. The parameters of the following equations are:

- mi the mass of body i

- vi the speed of body i

- ω the angular velocity of body

- I the moment of inertia

- L the angular momentum

- $\vec{N}$ the torque around axis

Linear momentum

$$\frac{d(mv)}{dt} = \sum_{i=1}^{N} f_i$$

$$L = \sum_{i=1}^{N} m_i r_i \times v_i$$

$$\vec{N} = \frac{dL}{dt}\vec{n} = I\frac{d\omega}{dt}\vec{n}$$

Angular momentum and Torque

For Multibody simulation, the input parameters are, for each body, the mass, the length and main geometric properties, the joint with other bodies, the constraints, etc. Then a motion or initial torque or movement is applied and the dynamic behavior is studied.

Multibody inputs and outputs depend on the case of study. Most of the time, the output of multibody simulation is the kinematic evolution of the system, the dynamic properties of the system (torque on joints, for instance) or the initial force or torque needed (for instance, it can allow the optimization of the PID controller of an electric engine).

Inputs:

- Body's mass mi

- Body's velocity v_i

- Body's moment of inertia I_i

- Body length L_i

- Joint static tensor $\{\tau_{i/j}\}$

- Initial torque or translation $\{\tau_o(t)\}$

Outputs:

- Body's angle evolution $\theta_i(t)$

- Body's gravity center coordinates $\{X_i(t)\}$

- Joint dynamic evolution $\{\tau_j(t)\}$

b) Fatigue Simulation

Fatigue analysis is a simulation performed using finite elements method. It aims at studying the behavior of a model subjected to a high number of cycles. Consequently, the number of cycles of the model is an input depending on the company's requirements. Moreover, the initial material properties and model shape are provided. Finally, a load case has to be applied on the model in order to analyze the mechanical behavior of the structure. The parameters of the following equations are:

- $[\sigma]$ the stress tensor

- $[\varepsilon]$ the deformation tensor

- v the Poisson's coefficient

- E the Young's modulus

- ρ the density of the material

- Nf the number of cycles

- b the fatigue strength exponent (Basquin's exponent)

- c the fatigue ductility exponent

- σf the fatigue strength coefficient

- εf the fatigue ductility coefficient

- σe the equivalent stress (when yielding occurs)

Stress Life vs. Strain Life

$$\frac{\Delta \varepsilon}{2} = \frac{\sigma_f}{E}.\left(2N_f\right)^b + \varepsilon_f.\left(2N_f\right)^c$$

Von-Mises yield criterion

$$\sigma_e = \left(\frac{1}{2}\left[\left(\sigma_x - \sigma_y\right)^2 + \left(\sigma_y - \sigma_z\right)^2 + \left(\sigma_z - \sigma_x\right)^2 + 6\left(\sigma_{xy}^2 + \sigma_{yz}^2 + \sigma_{xz}^2\right)\right]\right)^{\frac{1}{2}}$$

Tresca yield criterion

$$\sigma_e = \max\left(\left|\sigma_1 - \sigma_2\right|, \left|\sigma_2 - \sigma_3\right|, \left|\sigma_3 - \sigma_1\right|\right) \text{ with } \sigma_1, \sigma_2, \sigma_3 \text{ the principal stresses}$$

For digital Fatigue simulation, load cases are applied. They can be punctual forces (in N), torques (in N.m), distributed pressure (in N.m2) or a combination of these load cases. Consequently, the input parameter is a force or a pressure (or both). Also, the material properties of the FEA model are provided: density, Young's modulus, Poisson's ratio, shear modulus, etc. Finally, the number of cycles is required to perform the fatigue analysis. The output of Fatigue analysis is the stress or the strain on the structure. Depending on the requirements, the material properties and/or geometry are modified in order to guarantee a maximum displacement of structures.

Inputs:

- Stress $[\sigma]$ (or pressure distribution P)

-Young's modulus of the material E

-Reference density of the material ρ

-Poisson's coefficient of the material v

-Shear modulus G

-Number of cycles N

Outputs:

-Strain (or displacement) $[\varepsilon]$

Reihe Informationsmanagement im Engineering Karlsruhe (ISSN 1860-5990)

Herausgeber
Karlsruher Institut für Technologie
Institut für Informationsmanagement im Ingenieurwesen (IMI)
o. Prof. Dr. Dr.-Ing. Dr. h.c. Jivka Ovtcharova

Band
1 – 2005

Seidel, Michael
Methodische Produktplanung. Grundlagen, Systematik und Anwendung im Produktentstehungsprozess. 2005
ISBN 3-937300-51-1

Band
1 – 2006

Prieur, Michael
Functional elements and engineering template-based product development process. Application for the support of stamping tool design. 2006
ISBN 3-86644-033-2

Band
2 – 2006

Geis, Stefan Rafael
Integrated methodology for production related risk management of vehicle electronics (IMPROVE). 2006
ISBN 3-86644-011-1

Band
1 – 2007

Gloßner, Markus
Integrierte Planungsmethodik für die Presswerkneutypplanung in der Automobilindustrie. 2007
ISBN 978-3-86644-179-8

Band
2 – 2007

Mayer-Bachmann, Roland
Integratives Anforderungsmanagement. Konzept und Anforderungsmodell am Beispiel der Fahrzeugentwicklung. 2008
ISBN 978-3-86644-194-1

Band
1 – 2008

Mbang Sama, Achille
Holistic integration of product, process and resources integration in the automotive industry using the example of car body design and production. Product design, process modeling, IT implementation and potential benefits. 2008
ISBN 978-3-86644-243-6

Band
2 – 2008

Weigt, Markus
Systemtechnische Methodenentwicklung : Diskursive Definition heuristischer prozeduraler Prozessmodelle als Beitrag zur Bewältigung von informationeller Komplexität im Produktleben. 2008
ISBN 978-3-86644-285-6

Die Bände sind unter www.ksp.kit.edu als PDF frei verfügbar oder als Druckausgabe bestellbar.

Reihe Informationsmanagement im Engineering Karlsruhe (ISSN 1860-5990)

Herausgeber
Karlsruher Institut für Technologie
Institut für Informationsmanagement im Ingenieurwesen (IMI)
o. Prof. Dr. Dr.-Ing. Dr. h.c. Jivka Ovtcharova

Band
1 – 2009

Krappe, Hardy
Erweiterte virtuelle Umgebungen zur interaktiven, immersiven
Verwendung von Funktionsmodellen. 2009
ISBN 978-3-86644-380-8

Band
2 – 2009

Rogalski, Sven
Entwicklung einer Methodik zur Flexibilitätsbewertung von Produk-
tionssystemen. Messung von Mengen-, Mix- und Erweiterungs-
flexibilität zur Bewältigung von Planungsunsicherheiten in der
Produktion. 2009
ISBN 978-3-86644-383-9

Band
3 – 2009

Forchert, Thomas M.
Prüfplanung. Ein neues Prozessmanagement für Fahrzeugprüfungen.
2009
ISBN 978-3-86644-385-3

Band
1 – 2011

Erkayhan, Şeref
Ein Vorgehensmodell zur automatischen Kopplung von Services
am Beispiel der Integration von Standardsoftwaresystemen. 2011
ISBN 978-3-86644-697-7

Band
2 – 2011

Meier, Gunter
Prozessintegration des Target Costings in der Fertigungsindustrie
am Beispiel Sondermaschinenbau. 2011
ISBN 978-3-86644-679-3

Band
1 – 2012

Stanev, Stilian
Methodik zur produktionsorientierten Produktanalyse für die
Wiederverwendung von Produktionssystemen – 2REUSE. 2012
ISBN 978-3-86644-932-9

Band
2 – 2012

Wuttke, Fabian
Robuste Auslegung von Mehrkörpersystemen. Frühzeitige
Robustheitsoptimierung von Fahrzeugmodulen im Kontext
modulbasierter Entwicklungsprozesse. 2012
ISBN 978-3-86644-896-4

Die Bände sind unter www.ksp.kit.edu als PDF frei verfügbar oder als Druckausgabe bestellbar.

Reihe Informationsmanagement im Engineering Karlsruhe (ISSN 1860-5990)

Herausgeber
Karlsruher Institut für Technologie
Institut für Informationsmanagement im Ingenieurwesen (IMI)
o. Prof. Dr. Dr.-Ing. Dr. h.c. Jivka Ovtcharova

Band
3 – 2012

Katicic, Jurica
Methodik für Erfassung und Bewertung von emotionalem Kundenfeedback für variantenreiche virtuelle Produkte in immersiver Umgebung. 2012
ISBN 978-3-86644-930-5

Band
1 – 2013

Loos, Manuel Norbert
Daten- und termingesteuerte Entscheidungsmethodik der Fabrikplanung unter Berücksichtigung der Produktentstehung. 2013
ISBN 978-3-86644-963-3

Band
2 – 2013

Syal, Gagan
CAE - PROCESS AND NETWORK: A methodology for continuous product validation process based on network of various digital simulation methods. 2013
ISBN 978-3-7315-0090-2

Die Bände sind unter www.ksp.kit.edu als PDF frei verfügbar oder als Druckausgabe bestellbar.